DATE DUE

DE 1 6 '08			

DEMCO 38-296

English as a global language

David Crystal, world authority on the English language, has written a timely and informative account of the phenomenon of English as a global language. It includes a historical summary of the global development of English; an analysis, well supported by facts and figures, of the current spread and status of English as a first and second language internationally; and an informed assessment – by one of the leading scholars of language – of the future of English. The book asks three basic questions: what makes a world language? why is English the leading candidate? and will it continue to hold that position? It steers evenhandedly through the minefield of political debate about the current hegemony of English, and will appeal to anyone with an interest in language issues, whatever the political views on the subject.

English as a global language

DAVID CRYSTAL

CAMBRIDGE
UNIVERSITY PRESS

PUBLISHED BY THE PRESS SYNDICATE OF THE UNIVERSITY OF CAMBRIDGE
The Pitt Building, Trumpington Street, Cambridge CB2 1RP, United Kingdom

CAMBRIDGE UNIVERSITY PRESS
The Edinburgh Building, Cambridge CB2 2RU, United Kingdom
40 West 20th Street, New York, NY 10011–4211, USA
10 Stamford Road, Oakleigh, Melbourne 3166, Australia

© Cambridge University Press 1997

First published 1997

Printed in the United Kingdom at the University Press, Cambridge

Typeset in Galliard 10.5/13 pt

*A catalogue record for this book is available from
the British Library*

Library of Congress cataloguing in publication data
Crystal, David, 1941–
English as a global language / by David Crystal.
p.   cm.
Includes bibliographical references and index.
ISBN 0 521 59247 X (hb)
1. English language – Social aspects – Foreign countries.
2. English language – Social aspects – English-speaking countries.
3. Communication, International. 4. Intercultural communication.
5. Language and culture. 6. Language, Universal. I. Title.
PE2751.C79 1997
420–dc21   97–5003   CIP

ISBN 0 521 59247 X

Contents

Contents

Preface

It has all happened so quickly. In 1950, any notion of English as a true world language was but a dim, shadowy, theoretical possibility, surrounded by the political uncertainties of the Cold War, and lacking any clear definition or sense of direction. Fifty years on, and World English exists as a political and cultural reality. How could such a dramatic linguistic shift have taken place, in less than a lifetime? And why has English, and not some other language, achieved such a status? These are the questions which this book seeks to answer.

The time is right to address these issues. Thanks to progress in sociolinguistics, we now know a great deal about the social and cultural circumstances which govern language status and change, and several encyclopedic surveys have made available detailed information about world language use. There is also an increasingly urgent need for sensitive discussion. In several countries, the role of English has become politically contentious, and arguments have raged about its current and future status. Have matters developed to the point where the rise of English as a world language is unstoppable? To debate this question, we need to be aware of the factors which will influence the outcome.

It is difficult to write a book on this topic without it being interpreted as a political statement. Because there is no more intimate or more sensitive an index of identity than language, the subject is easily politicized, as it has been in such diverse locations as India, Malaysia, and the USA. A detached account is all the more desirable, and this is what I have tried to write in these pages, partly based on the historical research I carried out for my *Cambridge Encyclopedia of the English Language,* but extending this to provide a fuller and more focused analysis of the cultural factors involved. I have thus tried to tell the story of World English objectively, without taking sides on political issues, and without adopting the kind of triumphalist tone which is unfortunately all too common when people write on English in English.

But authors should always tell their readership where they stand, when dealing with contentious topics, hence the following summary. I firmly believe in two linguistic principles, which some people see as contradictory, but which for me are two sides of the one coin.

• I believe in the fundamental value of multilingualism, as an amazing world resource which presents us with different perspectives and insights, and thus enables us to reach a more profound understanding of the nature of the human mind and spirit. In my ideal world, everyone would be at least bi-lingual. I myself live in a community where two languages – Welsh and English – exist side by side, and I have cause to reflect every day on the benefits which come from being part of two cultures. A large part of my academic life, as a researcher in general linguistics, has been devoted to persuading people to take language and languages seriously, so that as much as possible of our linguistic heritage can be preserved.

• I believe in the fundamental value of a common language, as an amazing world resource which presents us with unprecedented possibilities for mutual understanding, and thus enables us to find fresh opportunities for international cooperation. In my ideal world, everyone would have fluent command of a single world language. I am already in the fortunate position of being a fluent user of the language which is most in contention for this role, and have cause to reflect every day on the benefits of having it at my disposal. A large part of my academic life, as a specialist in applied English linguistics, has been devoted to making these benefits available to others, so that the legacy of an unfavoured linguistic heritage should not lead inevitably to disadvantage.

We need to take both principles on board if we are to make any progress towards the kind of peaceful and tolerant society which most people dream about. The first principle fosters historical identity and promotes a climate of mutual respect. The second principle fosters cultural opportunity and promotes a climate of international intelligibility. I hate it when people turn these principles against each other, seeing them as contradictory rather than complementary; but I can perfectly well understand why it happens. I am no innocent in the real bilingual world. Living in a bilingual community as I do, and (when I'm not being a linguist) being the director of a bicultural arts centre, I am very well aware of the problems posed by limited financial resources, conflicts of interest, and downright intolerance. I have had my share of heated arguments with government authorities, local politicians, and national grant-awarding bodies over the question of how to arrive at a sensible and sensitive balance between the two principles, in their local application to the situation in Wales. So I am under no illusions about how difficult it is to achieve a consensus on such deep-rooted matters. But a search for balance and consensus there must always be, in a civilized society, and this need becomes even more critical at a world level, where the resources for mutual harm, as a consequence of failure, are so much greater.

I have written *English as a Global Language* as a contribution towards this long-term goal, but I cannot take the credit for first seeing the need for such a book. The suggestion in fact came from Mauro E. Mujica, chairman of US English, the largest organization which has been campaigning for English to be made the official language of the USA. He wanted to have a book which would explain to the members of his organization, in a succinct and factual way, and without political bias, why English has achieved such a worldwide status. I could not find such a book, nor did my own previous accounts of the history of the language give a comprehensive account of the social-historical factors involved. I therefore decided to research a short account for private circulation among his membership, and the present book is a heavily reworked, retitled, and much expanded version of that – now including, for example, a separate section on the 'official English' debate in the USA and further material on the use of English on the Internet. Many other revisions derive from suggestions made by a group of British and American academic reviewers of the typescript, commissioned by my publisher, Cambridge University Press, about ways in which the range and balance of the book might be improved; and *English as a Global Language* has benefited greatly from their input. I am also grateful to Randolph Quirk, especially for his suggestions about ways of improving the statistical picture presented in chapter 2, and to Geoffrey Nunberg for comments which have helped my understanding of the US situation, and for sending me some unpublished observations relating to the Internet, for use in chapter 4.

For some, of course, the mere mention of any political organ-ization, in the natural history of a project, is enough to bias its content. I should therefore make it very clear that this book has not been written according to any political agenda. I would have written exactly the same work if the initial idea had come from an organization on the other side of the US political linguistic divide. *English as a Global Language* simply asks three questions: what makes a world language? why is English the leading candidate? and will it continue to hold this position? An account of the relevant facts and factors can be of benefit to anyone with an interest in language matters, whatever their political views, and it is this which I hope the book has been able to achieve.

David Crystal
Holyhead

1

Why a global language?

'English is the global language.'

A headline of this kind must have appeared in a thousand newspapers and magazines in recent years. It is the kind of statement which seems so obvious that most people would give it hardly a second thought. Of course English is a global language, they would say. You hear it on television spoken by politicians from all over the world. Wherever you travel, you see English signs and advertisements. Indeed, if there is anything to wonder about at all, they might add, it is why such a headline should still be newsworthy.

But English **is** news. The language continues to make news daily in many countries. And the headline **isn't** stating the obvious. For what does it mean, exactly? Is it saying that everyone in the world speaks English? This is certainly not true. Is it saying, then, that every country in the world recognizes English as an official language? This is not true either. So what does it mean to say that a language is a global language? Why is English the language which is usually cited in this connection? How did the situation arise? And could it change? Or is it the case that, once a language becomes a global language, it is there for ever?

These are fascinating questions to explore, whether your first language is English or not. If English is your mother tongue, you may have mixed feelings about the way English is spreading around the world. You may feel pride, that your language is the one which has been so successful; but your pride may be tinged with concern, when you realize that people in other countries may not want to use the language in the same way that you do, and are changing it to suit themselves. We are all sensitive to the way other people use (or, it is more often said, abuse) 'our' language.

And if English is not your mother tongue, you may still have mixed feelings about it. You may be strongly motivated to learn it, because you know it will put you in touch with more people than any other language; but at the same time you know it will take a great deal of effort to master it, and you may begrudge that effort. Having made progress, you will feel pride in your achievement, and savour the communicative power you have at your disposal, but may none the less feel that mother-tongue speakers of English have an unfair advantage over you. And if you live in a country where the survival of your own language is threatened by the success of English, you may feel envious, resentful, or angry.

These feelings are natural, and would arise whichever language emerged as a global language. They are feelings which give rise to fears, whether real or imaginary, and fears lead to conflict. Language marches, language hunger-strikes, language rioting and language deaths are a fact, in several countries. Political differences over language economics, education, laws and rights are a daily encounter for millions. Language is always in the news, and the nearer a language moves to becoming a global language, the more newsworthy it is. So how does a language come to achieve global status?

What is a global language?

A language achieves a genuinely global status when it develops a special role that is recognized in every country. This might seem like stating the obvious, but it is not, for the notion of 'special role' has many facets. Such a role will be most evident in countries where large numbers of the people speak the language as a mother tongue – in the case of English, this would mean the

USA, Canada, Britain, Ireland, Australia, New Zealand, South Africa and several Caribbean countries. However, no language has ever been spoken by a mother-tongue majority in more than a few countries (Spanish leads, in this respect, in some twenty countries, chiefly in Latin America), so mother-tongue use by itself cannot give a language global status. To achieve such a status, a language has to be taken up by other countries around the world. They must decide to give it a special place within their communities, even though they may have few (or no) mother-tongue speakers.

There are two main ways in which this can be done. Firstly, a language can be made the official language of a country, to be used as a medium of communication in such domains as government, the law courts, the media, and the educational system. To get on in these societies, it is essential to master the official language as early in life as possible. Such a language is often described as a 'second language', because it is seen as a complement to a person's mother tongue, or 'first language'. The role of an official language is today best illustrated by English, which now has some kind of special status in over seventy countries, such as Ghana, Nigeria, India, Singapore and Vanuatu. (A complete list is given at the end of chapter 2.) This is far more than the status achieved by any other language – though French, German, Spanish, Russian, and Arabic are among those which have also developed a considerable official use. Each year brings new political decisions on the matter: for example, Rwanda gave English official status in 1996.

Secondly, a language can be made a priority in a country's foreign-language teaching, even though this language has no official status. It becomes the language which children are most likely to be taught when they arrive in school, and the one most available to adults who – for whatever reason – never learned it, or learned it badly, in their early educational years. Russian, for example, held privileged status for many years among the countries of the former Soviet Union. Mandarin Chinese continues to play an important role in South-east Asia. English is now the language most widely taught as a foreign language – in over 100 countries, such as China, Russia, Germany, Spain, Egypt and

3

Brazil – and in most of these countries it is emerging as the chief foreign language to be encountered in schools, often displacing another language in the process. In 1996, for example, English replaced French as the chief foreign language in schools in Algeria (a former French colony).

In reflecting on these observations, it is important to note that there are several ways in which a language can be official. It may be the sole official language of a country, or it may share this status with other languages. And it may have a 'semi-official' status, being used only in certain domains, or taking second place to other languages while still performing certain official roles. Many countries formally acknowledge a language's status in their constitution (e.g. India); some make no special mention of it (e.g. Britain). In certain countries, the question of whether the special status should be legally recognized is a source of considerable controversy – notably, in the USA (see chapter 5).

Similarly, there is great variation in the reasons for choosing a particular language as a favoured foreign language: they include historical tradition, political expediency, and the desire for commercial, cultural or technological contact. Also, even when chosen, the 'presence' of the language can vary greatly, depending on the extent to which a government or foreign-aid agency is prepared to give adequate financial support to a language-teaching policy. In a well-supported environment, resources will be devoted to helping people have access to the language and to learn it, through the media, libraries, schools, and institutes of higher education. There will be an increase in the number and quality of teachers able to teach the language. Books, tapes, computers, telecommunication systems and all kinds of teaching materials will be increasingly available. In many countries, however, lack of government support, or a shortage of foreign aid, has hindered the achievement of language-teaching goals.

Because of this three-pronged development – of first-language, official-language, and foreign-language speakers – it is inevitable that a global language will eventually come to be used by more people than any other language. English has already reached this stage. The statistics collected in chapter 2 suggest that nearly a quarter of the world's population is already fluent or competent in English, and this figure is steadily growing – in the late-1990s, that means between 1.2 and 1.5 billion people. No other language can match this growth. Even Chinese, found in eight different spoken languages, but unified by a common writing system, is known to only some 1.1 billion.

What makes a global language?

Why a language becomes a global language has little to do with the number of people who speak it. It is much more to do with who those speakers are. Latin became an international language throughout the Roman Empire, but this was not because the Romans were more numerous than the peoples they subjugated. They were simply more powerful. And later, when Roman military power declined, Latin remained for a millennium as the international language of education, thanks to a different sort of power – the ecclesiastical power of Roman Catholicism.

There is the closest of links between language dominance and cultural power, and this relationship will become increasingly clear as the history of English is told (see chapters 2–4). Without a strong power-base, whether political, military or economic, no language can make progress as an international medium of communication. Language has no independent existence, living in some sort of mystical space apart from the people who speak it. Language exists only in the brains and mouths and ears and hands and eyes of its users. When they succeed, on the international stage, their language succeeds. When they fail, their language fails.

This point may seem obvious, but it needs to be made at the outset, because over the years many popular and misleading beliefs have grown up about why a language should become internationally successful. It is quite common to hear people claim that a language is a paragon, on account of its perceived aesthetic qualities, clarity of expression, literary power, or religious standing. Hebrew, Greek, Latin, Arabic and French are among those which at various times have been lauded in such terms, and English is no exception. It is often suggested, for example, that there must be something inherently beautiful or logical about the structure of English, in order to explain why it is now so widely used. 'It has less grammar than other languages', some have suggested. 'English doesn't have a lot of endings on its words, nor do we have to remember the difference between masculine, feminine, and neuter gender, so it must be easier to learn'. In 1848, a reviewer in the British periodical *The Athenaeum* wrote:

In its easiness of grammatical construction, in its paucity of inflection, in its almost total disregard of the distinctions of gender excepting those of nature, in the simplicity and precision of its terminations and auxiliary verbs, not less than in the majesty, vigour and copiousness of its expression, our mother-tongue seems well adapted by *organization* to become the language of the world.

Such arguments are misconceived. Latin was once a major international language, despite its many inflectional endings and gender differences. French, too, has been such a language, despite its nouns being masculine or feminine; and so – at different times and places – have the heavily inflected Greek, Arabic, Spanish and Russian. Ease of learning has nothing to do with it. Children of all cultures learn to talk over more or less the same period of time, regardless of the differences in the grammar of their languages.

This is not to deny that a language may have certain properties which make it internationally appealing. For example, learners sometimes comment on the 'familiarity' of English vocabulary, deriving from the way English has over the centuries borrowed thousands of new words from the languages with which it has been in contact. The 'welcome' given to foreign vocabulary places English in contrast to some languages (notably, French) which have tried to keep it out, and gives it a cosmopolitan character which many see as an advantage for a global language. From a lexical point of view, English is in fact more a Romance than a Germanic language. And there have been comments made about other structural aspects, too, such as the absence in English grammar of a system of coding social class differences, which can make the language appear more 'democratic' to those who speak a language (e.g. Javanese) that does express an intricate system of class relationships. But these supposed traits of appeal are

6

incidental, and need to be weighed against linguistic features which would seem to be internationally much less desirable – notably, in the case of English, the many irregularities of its spelling system.

A language does not become a global language because of its intrinsic structural properties, or because of the size of its vocabulary, or because it has been a vehicle of a great literature in the past, or because it was once associated with a great culture or religion. These are all factors which can motivate someone to learn a language, of course, but none of them alone, or in combination, can ensure a language's world spread. Indeed, such factors cannot even guarantee survival as a living language – as is clear from the case of Latin, learned today as a classical language by only a scholarly and religious few. Correspondingly, inconvenient structural properties (such as awkward spelling) do not stop a language achieving international status either.

A language becomes an international language for one chief reason: the political power of its people – especially their military power. The explanation is the same throughout history. Why did Greek become a language of international communication in the Middle East over 2,000 years ago? Not because of the intellects of Plato and Aristotle: the answer lies in the swords and spears wielded by the armies of Alexander the Great. Why did Latin become known throughout Europe? Ask the legions of the Roman Empire. Why did Arabic come to be spoken so widely across northern Africa and the Middle East? Follow the spread of Islam, carried along by the force of the Moorish armies from the eighth century. Why did Spanish, Portuguese, and French find their way into the Americas, Africa and the Far East? Study the colonial policies of the Renaissance kings and queens, and the way these policies were ruthlessly implemented by armies and navies all over the known world. The history of a global language can be traced through the successful expeditions of its soldier/sailor speakers. And English, as we shall see in chapter 2, has been no exception.

But international language dominance is not solely the result of military might. It may take a militarily powerful nation to establish a language, but it takes an economically powerful one to maintain and expand it. This has always been the case, but it became a particularly critical factor early in the twentieth century, with economic developments beginning to operate on a global scale, supported by the new communication technologies – telegraph, telephone, radio – and fostering the emergence of massive multinational organizations. The growth of competitive industry and business brought an explosion of international marketing and advertising. The power of the press reached unprecedented levels, soon to be surpassed by the broadcasting media, with their ability to cross national boundaries with electromagnetic ease. Technology, in the form of movies and records, fuelled new mass entertainment industries which had a worldwide impact. The drive to make progress in science and technology fostered an international intellectual and research environment which gave scholarship and further education a high profile.

Any language at the centre of such an explosion of international activity would suddenly have found itself with a global status. And English, as we shall see in chapters 3 and 4, was in the right place at the right time. By the beginning of the nineteenth century, Britain had become the world's leading industrial and trading country. By the end of the century, the population of the USA (then approaching 100 million) was larger than that of any of the countries of western Europe, and its economy was the most productive and the fastest growing in the world. British political imperialism had sent English around the globe, during the nineteenth century, so that it was 'a language on which the sun never sets'. During the twentieth century, this world presence was maintained and promoted, almost single-handedly, through the economic supremacy of the new American superpower. And the language behind the US dollar was English.

Why do we need a global language?

Translation has played a central (though often unrecognized) role in human interaction for thousands of years. When monarchs or ambassadors met on the international stage, there would invariably be interpreters present. But there are limits to what can be done in this way. The more a community is linguistically mixed, the less it can rely on individuals to ensure communication between different groups. In communities where only two or three languages are in contact, bilingualism (or trilingualism) is a possible solution, for most young children can acquire more than one language with unselfconscious ease. But in communities where there are many languages in contact, as in much of Africa and South-east Asia, such a natural solution does not readily apply.

The problem has traditionally been solved by finding a language to act as a *lingua franca*, or 'common language'. Sometimes, when communities begin to trade with each other, they communicate by adopting a simplified language, known as a *pidgin*, which combines elements of their different languages. Many such pidgin languages survive today in territories which formerly belonged to the European colonial nations, and act as lingua francas; for example, West African Pidgin English is used extensively between several ethnic groups along the West African coast. Sometimes an indigenous language emerges as a lingua franca – usually the language of the most powerful ethnic group in the area, as in the case of Mandarin Chinese. The other groups then learn this language with varying success, and thus become to some degree bilingual. But most often, a language is accepted from outside the community, such as English or French, because of the political, economic, or religious influence of a foreign power.

The geographical extent to which a lingua franca can be used is entirely governed by political factors. Many lingua francas extend over quite small domains – between a few ethnic groups in one part of a single country, or linking the trading populations of just a few countries, as in the West African case. By contrast, Latin was a lingua franca throughout the whole of the Roman Empire – at least, at the level of government (very few 'ordinary' people in the subjugated domains would have spoken much Latin). And in modern times Swahili, Arabic, Spanish, French, English, Hindi, Portuguese and several other languages have developed a major international role as a lingua franca, in limited areas of the world.

The prospect that a lingua franca might be needed for the

whole world is something which has emerged strongly only in the twentieth century, and since the 1950s in particular. The chief international forum for political communication – the United Nations – dates only from 1945. Since then, many international bodies have come into being, such as the World Bank (also 1945), UNESCO and UNICEF (both 1946), the World Health Organization (1948) and the International Atomic Energy Agency (1957). Never before have so many countries (over 180, in the case of some UN bodies) been represented in single meeting-places. At a more restricted level, multinational regional or political groupings have come into being, such as the Commonwealth and the European Union. The pressure to adopt a single lingua franca, to facilitate communication in such contexts, is considerable, the alternative being expensive and impracticable multi-way translation facilities.

Usually a small number of languages have been designated official languages for an organization's activities: for example, the UN was established with five official languages – English, French, Spanish, Russian and Chinese. There is now a widespread view that it makes sense to try to reduce the numbers of languages involved in world bodies, if only to cut down on the vast amount of translation and clerical work required. Half the budget of an international organization can easily get swallowed up in translation costs. But trimming a translation budget is never easy, as obviously no country likes the thought of its language being given a reduced international standing. Language choice is always one of the most sensitive issues facing a planning committee. The ideal situation is one where a committee does not have to be involved – where all the participants at an international meeting automatically use a single language, as a utilitarian measure, because it is one which they have all come to learn for separate reasons. This situation seems to be slowly becoming a reality in meetings around the world, as general competence in English grows.

The need for a global language is particularly appreciated by the international academic and business communities, and it is here that the adoption of a single lingua franca is most in evidence, both in lecture-rooms and board-rooms, as well as in thousands of individual contacts being made daily all over the globe. A conversation over the Internet (see chapter 4) between academic physicists in Sweden, Italy, and India is at present practicable only if a common language is available. A situation where a Japanese company director arranges to meet German and Saudi Arabian contacts in a Singapore hotel to plan a multinational deal would not be impossible, if each plugged in to a 3-way translation support system, but it would be far more complicated than the alternative, which is for each to make use of the same language.

As these examples suggest, the growth in international contacts has been largely the result of two separate developments. The physicists would not be talking so conveniently to each other at all without the technology of modern communication. And the business contacts would be unable to meet so easily in Singapore without the technology of air transportation. The availability of both these facilities in the twentieth century has, more than anything else, provided the circumstances needed for a global language to grow.

People have, in short, become more mobile, both physically and electronically. Annual airline statistics show that steadily increasing numbers are finding the motivation as well as the means to transport themselves physically around the globe, and sales of faxes, modems, and personal computers show an even greater increase in those prepared to send their ideas in words and images electronically. It is now possible, using electronic mail, to copy a message to 100 locations all over the world virtually simultaneously. It is just as easy for me to send a message from my house in the small town of Holyhead, North Wales, to a friend in Washington as it is to get the same message to someone living just a few streets away from me. In fact, it is probably easier. That is why people so often talk, these days, of the 'global village'.

These trends would be taking place, presumably, if only a handful of countries were talking to each other. What has been so impressive about the developments which have taken place since the 1950s is that they have affected, to a greater or lesser extent, every country in the world, and that so many countries have come to be involved. There is no nation now which does not have some level of accessibility using telephone, radio, television, and air transport, though facilities such as fax, electronic mail and the Internet are much less widely available.

The scale and recency of the development has to be appreciated. In 1945, the United Nations began life with 51 member states. By 1956 this had risen to 80 members. But the independence movements which began at that time led to a massive increase in the number of new nations during the next decade, and this process continued steadily into the 1990s, following the collapse of the USSR. There were over 180 member states in 1996 – nearly three times as many as there were fifty years ago. And the trend may not yet be over, given the growth of so many regional nationalistic movements worldwide.

There are no precedents in human history for what happens to languages, in such circumstances of rapid change. There has never been a time when so many nations were needing to talk to each other so much. There has never been a time when so many people wished to travel to so many places. There has never been such a strain placed on the conventional resources of translating and interpreting. Never has the need for more widespread bilingualism been greater, to ease the burden placed on the professional few. And never has there been a more urgent need for a global language.

What are the dangers of a global language?

The benefits which would flow from the existence of a global language are considerable; but some commentators have pointed to possible risks. Perhaps a global language will cultivate an elite monolingual linguistic class, more complacent and dismissive in their attitudes towards other languages. Perhaps those who have such a language at their disposal – and especially those who have it as a mother-tongue – will be more able to think and work quickly in it, and to manipulate it to their own advantage at the expense of those who do not have it, thus maintaining in a linguistic guise the chasm between rich and poor. Perhaps the presence of a global language will make people lazy about learning other languages, or reduce their opportunities to do so.

Perhaps a global language will hasten the disappearance of minority languages, or – the ultimate threat – make **all** other languages unnecessary. 'A person needs only one language to talk to someone else', it is sometimes argued, 'and once a world language is in place, other languages will simply die away'. Linked with all this is the unpalatable face of linguistic triumphalism – the danger that some people will celebrate one language's success at the expense of others.

It is important to face up to these fears, and to recognize that they are widely held. There is no shortage of mother-tongue English speakers who believe in an evolutionary view of language ('let the fittest survive, and if the fittest happens to be English, then so be it') or who refer to the present global status of the language as a 'happy accident'. There are many who think that all language learning is a waste of time. And many more who see nothing wrong with the vision that a world with just one language in it would be a very good thing. For some, such a world would be one of unity and peace, with all misunderstanding washed away – a widely expressed hope underlying the movements in support of a universal artificial language (such as Esperanto). For others, such a world would be a desirable return to the 'innocence' that must have been present among human beings in the days before the Tower of Babel.

It is difficult to deal with anxieties which are so speculative, or, in the absence of evidence, to determine whether anything can be done to reduce or eliminate them. The last point can be quite briefly dismissed: the use of a single language by a community is no guarantee of social harmony or mutual understanding, as has been repeatedly seen in world history (e.g. the American Civil War, the Spanish Civil War, the Vietnam War, former Yugoslavia, contemporary Northern Ireland); nor does the presence of more than one language within a community necessitate civil strife, as seen in several successful examples of peaceful multilingual coexistence (e.g. Finland, Singapore, Switzerland). The other points, however, need to be taken more slowly, to appreciate the alternative perspective. The arguments are each illustrated with reference to English – but the same arguments would apply whatever language was in the running for global status.

- *Linguistic power*   Will those who speak a global language as a mother tongue automatically be in a position of power compared with those who have to learn it as an official or foreign language? The risk is certainly real. It is possible, for example, that scientists who do not have English as a mother tongue will take longer to assimilate reports in English compared with their mother-tongue colleagues, and will as a consequence have less time to carry out their own creative work. It is possible that people who write up their research in languages other than English will have their work ignored by the international community. It is possible that senior managers who do not have English as a mother tongue, and who find themselves working for English-language companies in such parts of the world as Europe or Africa, could find themselves at a disadvantage compared with their mother-tongue colleagues, especially when meetings involve the use of informal speech. There is already anecdotal evidence to suggest that these things happen.

However, if proper attention is paid to the question of language learning, the problem of disadvantage dramatically diminishes. If a global language is taught early enough, from the time that children begin their full-time education, and if it is maintained continuously and resourced well, the kind of linguistic competence which emerges in due course is a real and powerful bilingualism, indistinguishable from that found in any speaker who has encountered the language since birth. These are enormous 'ifs', with costly financial implications, and it is therefore not surprising that this kind of control is currently achieved by only a minority of non-native learners of any language; but the fact that it is achievable indicates that there is nothing inevitable about the disadvantage scenario.

It is worth reflecting, at this point, on the notion that children are born ready for bilingualism. Some two-thirds of the children on earth grow up in a bilingual environment, and develop competence in it. There is a naturalness with which they assimilate another language, once they are regularly exposed to it, which is the envy of adults. It is an ability which seems to die away as children reach their teens, and much academic debate has been devoted to the question of why this should be (the question of 'critical periods'). There is however widespread agreement that, if we want to take the task of foreign language learning seriously, the principle has to be 'the earlier the better'. And when that task **is** taken seriously, with reference to the acquisition of a global language, the elitism argument evaporates.

• *Linguistic complacency* Will a global language eliminate the motivation for adults to learn other languages? Here too the problem is real enough. Clear signs of linguistic complacency, common observation suggests, are already present in the archetypal British or American tourist who travels the world assuming that everyone speaks English, and that it is somehow the fault of the local people if they do not. The stereotype of an English tourist repeatedly asking a foreign waiter for tea in a loud 'read my lips' voice is too near the reality to be comfortable. There seems already to be a genuine, widespread lack of motivation to learn other languages, fuelled partly by lack of money and opportunity, but also by lack of interest, and this might well be fostered by the increasing presence of English as a global language.

It is important to appreciate that we are dealing here with questions of attitude or state of mind rather than questions of ability – though it is the latter which is often cited as the explanation. 'I'm no good at languages' is probably the most widely heard apology for not making any effort at all to acquire even a basic knowledge of a new language. Commonly, this self-denigration derives from an unsatisfactory language learning experience in school: the speaker is perhaps remembering a poor result in school examinations – which may reflect no more than an unsuccessful teaching approach or a not unusual breakdown in teacher–adolescent relationships. 'I never got on with my French teacher' is another typical comment. But this does not stop people going on to generalize that 'the British (or the Americans, etc.) are not very good at learning languages'.

These days, there are clear signs of growing awareness, within English-speaking communities, of the need to break away from the traditional monolingual bias. In economically hard-pressed

times, success in boosting exports and attracting foreign investment can depend on subtle factors, and sensitivity to the language
spoken by a country's potential foreign partners is known to be
particularly influential. At least at the levels of business and
industry, many firms have begun to make fresh efforts in this
direction. But at grass-roots tourist level, too, there are signs of a
growing respect for other cultures, and a greater readiness to
engage in language learning. Language attitudes are changing all
the time, and more and more people are discovering, to their
great delight, that they are not at all bad at picking up a foreign
language.

In particular, statements from influential politicians and administrators are beginning to be made which are helping to foster
a fresh climate of opinion about the importance of language
learning. A good example is an address given to the world
members' conference of the English-Speaking Union in 1996 by
the former secretary-general of the Commonwealth, Sir Sridath
Ramphal. His title, 'World language: opportunities, challenges,
responsibilities', itself contains a corrective to triumphalist
thinking, and his text repeatedly argues against it:

It is all too easy to make your way in the world linguistically with
English as your mother tongue . . . We become lazy about learning other
languages . . . We all have to make a greater effort. English may be the
world language; but it is not the world's only language and if we are to
be good global neighbours we shall have to be less condescending to the
languages of the world – more assiduous in cultivating acquaintance
with them.

It remains to be seen whether such affirmations of good will have
long-term effect. In the meantime, it is salutary to read some of
the comparative statistics about foreign language learning. For
example, a European business survey by Grant Thornton
reported in 1996 that 90 per cent of businesses in Belgium, The
Netherlands, Luxembourg and Greece had an executive able to
negotiate in another language, whereas only 38 per cent of British
companies had someone who could do so. The UK-based Centre
for Information on Language Teaching found that a third of
British exporters miss opportunities because of poor language

skills. And several studies have shown that English-monolingual companies are increasingly encountering language difficulties as they try to expand in those areas of the world thought to have greatest prospects of growth, such as East Asia, South America, and Eastern Europe – areas where English has traditionally had a relatively low presence. The issues are beginning to be addressed – for example, Australian schools now teach Japanese as the first foreign language, and both the USA and UK are now paying more attention to Spanish (which, in terms of mother-tongue use, is growing more rapidly than English) – but we are still a long way from a world where the economic and other arguments have universally persuaded the English-speaking nations to renounce their linguistic insularity.

• *Linguistic death* Will the emergence of a global language hasten the disappearance of minority languages and cause wide-spread language death? To answer this question, we must first establish a general perspective. The processes of language domination and loss have been known throughout linguistic history, and exist independently of the emergence of a global language. No one knows how many languages have died, since humans became able to speak, but it must be thousands. In many of these cases, the death has been caused by an ethnic group coming to be assimilated within a more dominant society, and adopting its language. The situation continues today, though the matter is being discussed with increasing urgency because of the unprecedented rate at which indigenous languages are being lost, especially in North America, Brazil, Australia, Indonesia and parts of Africa. Some estimates suggest that perhaps 80 per cent of the world's 6,000 or so living languages will die out within the next century.

If this happens, it will indeed be an intellectual and social tragedy. When a language dies, so much is lost. Especially in languages which have never been written down, or which have been written down only recently, language is the repository of the history of a people. It is their identity. Oral testimony, in the form of sagas, folktales, songs, rituals, proverbs, and many other practices, provides us with a unique view of our world and a unique canon of literature. It is their legacy to the rest of humanity. Once lost, it can never be recaptured. The argument is similar to that used in relation to the conservation of species and the environment. The conservation of languages is arguably also a priority, and it is good to see in the 1990s a number of international organizations being formed with the declared aim of recording for posterity as many endangered languages as possible.

However, the emergence of any one language as global has little to do with this unhappy state of affairs. Whether Sorbian survives in Germany or Galician in Spain has to do with the local political history of those countries, and with the regional dominance of German and Spanish respectively, and bears no immediate relationship to the standing of German or Spanish on the world stage. Nor is it easy to see how the arrival of English as a global language could directly influence the future of these or most other minority languages. An effect is likely only in those areas where English has itself come to be the dominant first language, such as in North America, Australia and the Celtic parts of the British Isles. The early history of language contact in these areas was indeed one of conquest and assimilation. But in more recent times, the emergence of English as a truly global language has, if anything, had the reverse effect – stimulating a stronger response in support of a local language than might otherwise have been the case. Movements for language rights (alongside civil rights in general) have played an important part in several countries, such as in relation to the Maori in New Zealand, the Aboriginal languages of Australia, the Indian languages of Canada and the USA, and some of the Celtic languages. Although often too late, in certain instances the decline of a language has been slowed, and occasionally (as in the case of Welsh) halted.

The existence of vigorous movements in support of linguistic minorities, commonly associated with nationalism, illustrates an important truth about the nature of language in general. The need for mutual intelligibility, which is part of the argument in favour of a global language, is only one side of the story. The other side is the need for identity – and people tend to underestimate the role of identity when they express anxieties about language injury and death. Language is a major means (some would say the chief means) of showing where we belong, and of distinguishing one social group from another, and all over the world we can see evidence of linguistic divergence rather than convergence. For decades, many people in the countries of former Yugoslavia made use of a common language, Serbo-Croatian. But since the civil wars of the early 1990s, the Serbs have begun to refer to their language as Serbian, the Bosnians to theirs as Bosnian, and the Croats to theirs as Croatian, with each side drawing attention to the linguistic features which are distinctive. A similar situation exists in Scandinavia, where Swedish, Norwegian, and Danish are largely mutually intelligible, but are none the less considered to be different languages.

Arguments about the need for national or cultural identity are often seen as being opposed to those about the need for mutual intelligibility. But this is misleading. It is perfectly possible to develop a situation in which intelligibility and identity happily co-exist. This situation is the familiar one of bilingualism – but a bilingualism where one of the languages within a speaker is the global language, providing access to the world community, and the other is a regional language, providing access to a local community. The two functions can be seen as complementary, responding to different needs. And it is because the functions are so different that a world of linguistic diversity can in principle continue to exist in a world united by a common language.

None of this is to deny that the emergence of a global language can influence the structure of other languages – especially by providing a fresh source of loan-words for use by these other languages. Such influences can be welcomed (in which case, peo-ple talk about their language being 'varied' and 'enriched') or opposed (in which case, the metaphors are those of 'injury' and 'death'). For example, in recent years, one of the healthiest languages, French, has tried to protect itself by law against what is widely perceived to be the malign influence of English: in official contexts, it is now illegal to use an English word where a French word already exists, even though the usage may have widespread popular support (e.g. *computer* for *ordinateur*). Purist commentators from several other countries have also expressed concern at the way in which English vocabulary – especially that of American English – has come to permeate their high streets and TV programmes. The arguments are carried on with great emotional force. Even though only a tiny part of the lexicon is ever affected in this way, that is enough to arouse the wrath of the prophets of doom. (They usually forget the fact that English itself, over the centuries, has borrowed thousands of words from other languages, and constructed thousands more from the elements of other languages – including *computer*, incidentally, which derives from Latin, the mother-language of French.)

Could anything stop a global language?

Any discussion of an emerging global language has to be seen in the political context of global governance as a whole. In January 1995, the Commission on Global Governance published its report, *Our Global Neighbourhood*. A year later, the Commission's co-chairman, Sridath Ramphal, commented (in the paper referred to above):

There were, for the most part, people who were pleased that the Report had engaged the central issue of a global community, but they took us to task for not going on – in as they thought in a logical way – to call for a world language. They could not see how the global neighbourhood, the global community, which they acknowledged had come into being, could function effectively without a world language. A neighbourhood that can only talk in the tongues of many was not a neighbourhood that was likely to be cohesive or, perhaps, even cooperative . . . And they were right in one respect; but they were wrong in the sense that we **have** a world language. It is not the language of imperialism; it is the language we have seen that has evolved out of a history of which we need not always be proud, but whose legacies we must use to good effect.

And at another place, he comments: 'there is no retreat from English as the world language; no retreat from an English-speaking world'.

Strong political statements of this kind immediately prompt the question, 'Could anything stop a language, once it achieves a global status?' The short answer must be 'yes'. If language dominance is a matter of political power, then a revolution in the balance of global power could have consequences for the choice of global language. There is no shortage of books – chiefly within the genre of science fiction – which foresee a future in which, following some cataclysmic scenario, the universal language is Chinese, Arabic or even some Alien tongue. But to end up with such a scenario, the revolution would indeed have to be cataclysmic, and it is difficult to speculate sensibly about what this might be. Smaller-scale revolutions in the world order would be unlikely to have much effect, given that – as we shall see in later chapters – English is now so widely established that it can no longer be thought of as 'owned' by any single nation.

A rather more plausible scenario is that an alternative method of communication could emerge which would eliminate the need for a global language. The chief candidate here is automatic translation ('machine translation'). If progress in this domain continues to be as rapid as it has been in the past decade, there is a distinct possibility that, within a generation or two, it will be routine for people to communicate with each other directly, using their first languages, with a computer 'taking the strain' between them. This state of affairs can already be seen, to a limited extent, on the Internet, where some firms are now offering a basic translation service between certain language pairs. A sender types in a message in language X, and a version of it appears on the receiver's screen in language Y. The need for post-editing is still considerable, however, as translation software is currently very limited in its ability to handle idiomatic, stylistic, and several other linguistic features; the machines are nowhere near replacing their human counterparts. Similarly, notwithstanding the remarkable progress in speech recognition and synthesis which has taken place in recent years, the state of the art in real-time speech-to-speech automatic translation is still primitive. The 'Babel fish', inserted into the ear, thus making all spoken languages (in the galaxy) intelligible, is no more than an intriguing concept (envisaged by Douglas Adams in *The Hitch-Hiker's Guide to the Galaxy*).

The accuracy and speed of real-time automatic translation is undoubtedly going to improve dramatically in the next twenty-five to fifty years, but it is going to take much longer before this medium becomes so globally widespread, and so economically accessible to all, that it poses a threat to the current availability and appeal of a global language. And during this time frame, all the evidence suggests that the position of English as a global language is going to become stronger. By the time automatic translation matures as a popular communicative medium, that position will very likely have become impregnable. It will be very interesting to see what happens then – whether the presence of a global language will eliminate the demand for world translation services, or whether the economics of automatic translation will so undercut the cost of global language learning that the latter will become otiose. It will be an interesting battle 100 years from now.

A critical era

It is impossible to make confident predictions about the emergence of a global language. There are no precedents for this kind of linguistic growth, other than on a much smaller scale. And the speed with which a global language scenario has arisen is truly remarkable. Within little more than a generation, we have moved from a situation where a world language was a theoretical possibility to one where it is a rapidly approaching reality.

No government has yet found it possible to plan confidently, in such circumstances. Languages of identity need to be maintained. Access to the emerging global language – widely perceived as a language of opportunity – needs to be guaranteed. Both principles demand massive resources. The irony is that the issue is approaching a climax at a time when the world financial climate can least afford it.

Fundamental decisions about priorities have to be made. Those making the decisions need to bear in mind that we may well be approaching a critical moment in human linguistic history. It is possible that a global language will emerge only once. Certainly, as we have seen, after such a language comes to be established it would take a revolution of world-shattering proportions to replace it. And in due course, the last quarter of the twentieth century will be seen as a critical time in the emergence of this global language.

For the reasons presented in the next three chapters, all the signs suggest that this global language will be English. But there is still some way to go before a genuinely global lingua franca becomes a reality. Despite the remarkable growth in the use of English, some two-thirds of the world population do not yet use it. In certain parts of the world (most of the states of the former Soviet Union, for example), English has still a very limited presence. And in some countries, increased resources are being devoted to maintaining the role of other languages (such as the use of French in several countries of Africa). Notwithstanding the general world trend, there are many linguistic battles still to be fought.

Governments who wish to play their part in influencing the world's linguistic future should therefore ponder carefully, as they make political decisions and allocate resources for language planning. Now, more than at any time in linguistic history, they need to adopt long-term views, and to plan ahead. If they miss this linguistic boat, there may be no other.

2
Why English?
The historical context

'Why is English the global language, and not some other?' There are two answers to the question: one is geographical-historical; the other is socio-cultural. The geo-historical answer shows how English reached a position of pre-eminence, and this is presented below. The socio-cultural answer explains why it remains so, and this is presented in chapters 3 and 4. The combination of these two strands has brought into existence a language which consists of many varieties, each distinctive in its use of sounds, grammar, and vocabulary, and the implications of this are presented in chapter 5.

The historical account traces the movement of English around the world, beginning with the pioneering voyages to the Americas, Asia, and the Antipodes. It was an expansion which continued with the nineteenth-century colonial developments in Africa and the South Pacific, and which took a significant further step when it was adopted in the mid twentieth century as an official or semi-official language by many newly independent states. English is now represented in every continent, and in islands of the three major oceans – Atlantic (St Helena), Indian (Seychelles) and Pacific (in many islands, such as Fiji and Hawaii). It is this spread of representation which makes the application of the label 'global language' a reality.

The socio-cultural explanation looks at the way people all over the world, in many walks of life, have come to depend on English for their well-being. The language has penetrated deeply into the international domains of political life, business, safety, communication, entertainment, the media and education. The convenience of having a lingua franca available to serve global human relations and needs has come to be appreciated by millions. Several domains, as we shall see, have come to be totally dependent on it – the computer software industry being a prime example. A language's future seems assured when so many organizations come to have a vested interest in it.

Origins

How far back do we have to go in order to find the origins of global English? In a sense, the language has always been on the move. As soon as it arrived in England from northern Europe, in the fifth century, it began to spread around the British Isles. It entered parts of Wales, Cornwall, Cumbria and southern Scotland, traditionally the strongholds of the Celtic languages. After the Norman invasion of 1066, many nobles from England fled north to Scotland, where they were made welcome, and eventually the language (in a distinctive Scots variety) spread throughout the Scottish lowlands. From the twelfth century, Anglo-Norman knights were sent across the Irish Sea, and Ireland gradually fell under English rule.

But, compared with later events, these were movements on a very local scale – within the British Isles. The first significant step in the progress of English towards its status as a global language did not take place for another 300 years, towards the end of the sixteenth century. At that time, the number of mother-tongue English speakers in the world is thought to have been between 5 and 7 million, almost all of them living in the British Isles. Between the end of the reign of Elizabeth I (1588) and the beginning of the reign of Elizabeth II (1952), this figure increased almost fiftyfold, to some 250 million, the vast majority living outside the British Isles. Most of these people were, and continue to be, Americans, and it is in sixteenth-century North America that we first find a fresh dimension being added to the history of the language.

America

The first expedition from England to the New World was com-missioned by Walter Raleigh in 1584, and proved to be a failure. A group of explorers landed near Roanoke Island, in what is now North Carolina, and established a small settlement. Conflict with the native people followed, and it proved necessary for a ship to return to England for help and supplies. By the time these arrived, in 1590, none of the original group of settlers could be found. The mystery of their disappearance has never been solved.

The first permanent English settlement dates from 1607, when an expedition arrived in Chesapeake Bay. The colonists called their settlement Jamestown (after James I) and the area Virginia (after the 'Virgin Queen', Elizabeth). Further settlements quickly followed along the coast, and also on the nearby islands, such as Bermuda. Then, in November 1620, the first group of Puritans, thirty-five members of the English Separatist Church, arrived on the *Mayflower* in the company of sixty-seven other settlers. Prevented by storms from reaching Virginia, they landed at Cape Cod Bay, and established a settlement at what is now Plymouth, Massachusetts.

The group was extremely mixed, ranging in age from young children to people in their 50s, and with diverse regional, social, and occupational backgrounds. What the 'Pilgrim Fathers' (as they were later called) had in common was their search for a land where they could found a new religious kingdom, free from persecution and 'purified' from the church practices they had experienced in England. It was a successful settlement, and by 1640 about 25,000 immigrants had come to the area.

The two settlements – one in Virginia, to the south, the other to the north, in present-day New England – had different linguistic backgrounds. The southern colonists came mainly from England's 'West Country' – such counties as Somerset and Gloucestershire – and brought with them its characteristic accent, with its 'Zummerzet' voicing of *s* sounds, and the *r* strongly pronounced after vowels. Echoes of this accent can still be heard in the speech of communities living in some of the isolated valleys and islands in the area, such as Tangier Island in Chesapeake Bay.

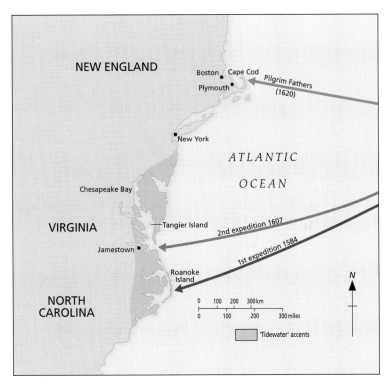

Early English-speaking settlement areas in America

These 'Tidewater' accents, as they are called, have changed somewhat over the past 300 years, but not as rapidly (because of the relative isolation of the speakers) as elsewhere in the country. They are sometimes said to be the closest we will ever get to the sound of Shakespeare's English.

By contrast, many of the Plymouth colonists came from counties in the east of England – in particular, Lincolnshire, Nottinghamshire, Essex, Kent and London, with some from the Midlands, and a few from further afield. These eastern accents were rather different – notably, lacking an *r* after vowels – and they proved to be the dominant influence in this area. The tendency 'not to pronounce the *r*' is still a feature of the speech of people from New England.

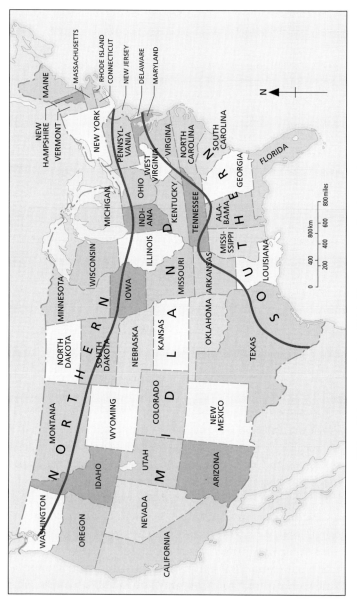

Major dialect areas in the USA: Northern, Midland, Southern

The later population movements across America largely preserved the dialect distinctions which arose out of these early patterns of settlement. The New England people moved west into the region of the Great Lakes; the southerners moved along the Gulf Coast and into Texas; and the midlanders spread throughout the whole of the vast, mid-western area, across the Mississippi and ultimately into California. The dialect picture was never a neat one, because of widespread north–south movements within the country, and the continuing inflow of immigrants from different parts of the world. There are many mixed dialect areas, and pockets of unexpected dialect forms. But the main divisions of north, midland, and south are still found throughout America today.

During the seventeenth century, new shiploads of immigrants brought an increasing variety of linguistic backgrounds into the country. Pennsylvania, for example, came to be settled mainly by Quakers whose origins were mostly in the Midlands and the north of England. People speaking very different kinds of English thus found themselves living alongside each other, as the 'middle' Atlantic areas (New York, in particular) became the focus of settlement. As a result, the sharp divisions between regional dialects gradually began to blur.

Then, in the eighteenth century, there was a vast wave of immigration from northern Ireland. The Irish had been migrating to America from around 1600, but the main movements took place during the 1720s, when around 50,000 Irish and Scots-Irish immigrants arrived. By the time independence was declared (1776), it is thought that one in seven of the colonial population was Scots-Irish. Many stayed along the coast, especially in the area of Philadelphia, but most moved inland through the mountains in search of land. They were seen as frontier people, with an accent which at the time was described as 'broad'. The opening up of the south and west was largely due to the pioneering spirit of this group of settlers.

By the time of the first census, in 1790, the population of the country was around 4 million, most of whom lived along the Atlantic coast. A century later, after the opening up of the west, the population numbered over 50 million, spread throughout the continent. The accent which emerged can now be heard all over the so-called Sunbelt (from Virginia to southern California), and is the accent most commonly associated with present-day American speech.

It was not only England which influenced the directions that the English language was to take in America. The Spanish had occupied large parts of the west and south-west. The French were present in the northern territories, around the St Lawrence River, and throughout the middle regions (French Louisiana) as far as the Gulf of Mexico. The Dutch were in New York (originally New Amsterdam) and the surrounding area. Large numbers of Germans began to arrive at the end of the seventeenth century, settling mainly in Pennsylvania and its hinterland. In addition, there were increasing numbers of Africans entering the south, as a result of the slave trade, and this dramatically increased in the eighteenth century: a population of little more than 2,500 black slaves in 1700 had become about 100,000 by 1775, far out-numbering the southern whites.

The nineteenth century saw a massive increase in American immigration, as people fled the results of revolution, poverty, and famine in Europe. Large numbers of Irish came following the potato famine in Ireland in the 1840s. Germans and Italians came, escaping the consequences of the failed 1848 revolutions. And, as the century wore on, there were increasing numbers of Central European Jews, especially fleeing from the pogroms of the 1880s. In the first two decades of the present century, immigrants were entering the USA at an average of three-quarters of a million a year. In 1900, the population was just over 75 million. This total had doubled by 1950.

Within one or two generations of arrival, most of these immi-grant families had come to speak English, through a natural process of assimilation. Grandparents and grandchildren found themselves living in very different linguistic worlds. The result was a massive growth in mother-tongue use of English. According to the 1990 census, the number of people (over five years of age) who spoke only English at home had grown to over 198 million – 86 per cent of the population. This was almost four times as many mother-tongue speakers as any other nation.

Some commentators have suggested that the English language was a major factor in maintaining American unity throughout this period of remarkable cultural diversification – a 'glue' which brought people together and a medium which gave them common access to opportunity. At the same time, some minority groups began to be concerned about the preservation of their cultural and linguistic heritage, within a society which was becoming increasingly monolingual. The seeds of a conflict between the need for intelligibility and the need for identity were beginning to grow – a conflict which, by the later decades of the twentieth century, had fuelled the movement in support of English as the official language of the USA (see chapter 5).

Canada

Meanwhile, the English language was making progress further north. The first English-language contact with Canada was as early as 1497, when John Cabot is thought to have reached Newfoundland; but English migration along the Atlantic coast did not develop until a century later, when the farming, fishing, and fur-trading industries attracted English-speaking settlers. There was ongoing conflict with the French, whose presence dated from the explorations of Jacques Cartier in the 1520s; but this came to an end when the French claims were gradually surrendered during the eighteenth century, following their defeat in Queen Anne's War (1702–13) and the French and Indian War (1754–63). During the 1750s thousands of French settlers were deported from Acadia (modern Nova Scotia), and were replaced by settlers from New England. The numbers were then further increased by many coming directly from England, Ireland, and Scotland (whose earlier interest in the country is reflected in the name *Nova Scotia* 'New Scotland').

The next major development followed the US Declaration of Independence in 1776. Loyalist supporters of Britain (the 'United Empire Loyalists') found themselves unable to stay in the new United States, and most left for Canada, settling first in what is now Nova Scotia, then moving to New Brunswick and further inland. They were soon followed by many thousands (the

31

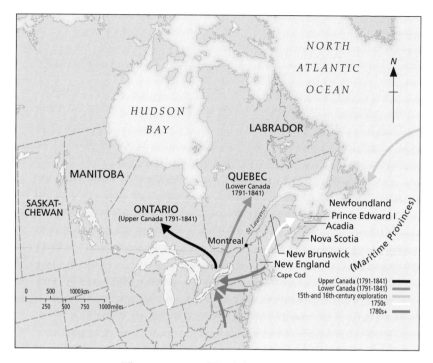

The movement of English into Canada

so-called 'late Loyalists') who were attracted by the cheapness of land, especially in the area known as Upper Canada (above Montreal and north of the Great Lakes). Within fifty years, the population of this province had reached 100,000.

Because of its origins, Canadian English has a great deal in common with the rest of the English spoken in North America, and those who live outside Canada often find it difficult to hear the difference. Many British people identify a Canadian accent as American; many Americans identify it as British. Canadians themselves insist on not being identified with either group, and certainly the variety does display a number of unique features. In addition, the presence of French as a co-official language, chiefly spoken in Quebec, produces a sociolinguistic situation not found in other English-speaking countries.

The Caribbean

During the early years of American settlement, the English language was also spreading in the south. A highly distinctive kind of speech was emerging in the islands of the West Indies and the southern part of the mainland, spoken by the incoming black population. This was a consequence of the importation of African slaves to work on the sugar plantations, a practice started by the Spanish as early as 1517.

From the early seventeenth century, ships from Europe travelled to the West African coast, where they exchanged cheap goods for black slaves. The slaves were shipped in barbarous conditions to the Caribbean islands and the American coast, where they were in turn exchanged for such commodities as sugar, rum, and molasses. The ships then returned to England, completing an 'Atlantic triangle' of journeys, and the process began again. The first twenty African slaves arrived in Virginia on a Dutch ship in 1619. By the time of the American Revolution (1776) their numbers had grown to half a million, and there were over 4 million by the time slavery was abolished, at the end of the US Civil War (1865).

The policy of the slave-traders was to bring people of different language backgrounds together in the ships, to make it difficult for groups to plot rebellion. The result was the growth of several pidgin forms of communication, and in particular a pidgin between the slaves and the sailors, many of whom spoke English. Once arrived in the Caribbean, this pidgin English continued to act as a means of communication between the black population and the new landowners, and among the blacks themselves. Then, when their children were born, the pidgin gradually began to be used as a mother tongue, producing the first black creole speech in the region.

It is this creole English which rapidly came to be used throughout the southern plantations, and in many of the coastal towns and islands. At the same time, standard British English was becoming a prestige variety throughout the area, because of the emerging political influence of Britain. Creole forms of French, Spanish and Portuguese were also developing in and around the

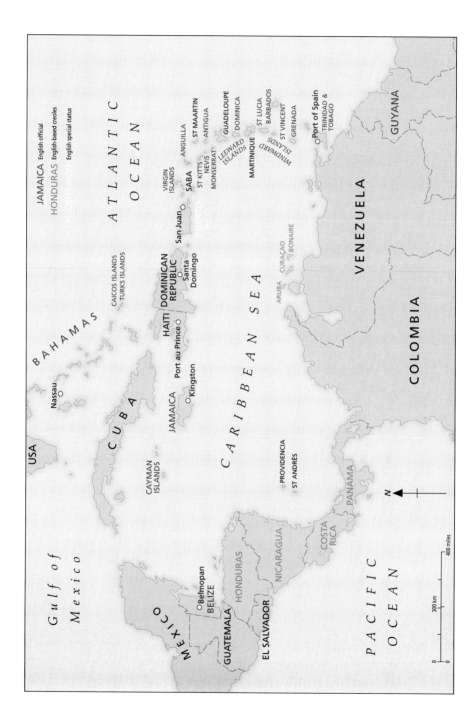

Caribbean, and some of these interacted with both the creole and the standard varieties of English. The Caribbean islands, and parts of the adjacent Central and South American mainland, thus came to develop a remarkably diverse range of varieties of English, reflecting their individual political and cultural histories. Moreover, West Indian speech did not stay within the Caribbean islands, but moved well outside, with large communities eventually found in Canada, the USA and Britain.

Australia and New Zealand

Towards the end of the eighteenth century, the continuing process of British world exploration established the English language in the southern hemisphere. The numbers of speakers have never been very large, by comparison with those in the northern hemisphere, but the varieties of English which have emerged are just as distinctive.

Australia was visited by James Cook in 1770, and within twenty years Britain had established its first penal colony at Sydney, thus relieving the pressure on the overcrowded prisons in England. About 130,000 prisoners were transported during the fifty years after the arrival of the 'first fleet' in 1788. 'Free' settlers, as they were called, also began to enter the country from the very beginning, but they did not achieve substantial numbers until the mid-nineteenth century. From then on, immigration rapidly increased. By 1850, the population of Australia was about 400,000, and by 1900 nearly 4 million. Today, it is nearly 18 million.

The British Isles provided the main source of settlers, and thus the main influence on the language. Many of the convicts came from London and Ireland (especially following the 1798 Irish rebellion), and features of the Cockney twang of London and the

(*Opposite*) The Caribbean Islands, showing (a) countries where Standard English is an official language; in these areas, English-based creoles are also widely used; (b) countries where a language other than English is the official language, but an English-based creole is none the less spoken. The special standing of US English in Puerto Rico is noted separately.

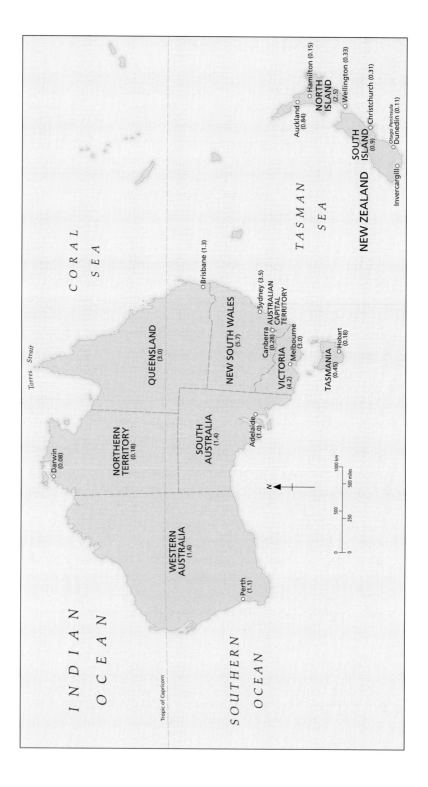

INDIAN OCEAN

Torres Strait

NORTHERN TERRITORY (0.18)

Darwin (0.08)

WESTERN AUSTRALIA (1.6)

Perth (1.1)

SOUTH AUSTRALIA (1.4)

Adelaide (1.0)

QUEENSLAND (3.0)

CORAL SEA

Brisbane (1.3)

NEW SOUTH WALES (5.7)

Sydney (3.5)

Canberra (0.28) AUSTRALIAN CAPITAL TERRITORY

VICTORIA (4.2)

Melbourne (3.0)

TASMANIA (0.45)

Hobart (0.18)

SOUTHERN OCEAN

Tropic of Capricorn

N

0   500
0   250   500 miles
1000 km

TASMAN SEA

NEW ZEALAND

NORTH ISLAND (2.5)

Auckland (0.84)

Hamilton (0.15)

Wellington (0.33)

SOUTH ISLAND (0.9)

Christchurch (0.31)

Otago Peninsula
Dunedin (0.11)

Invercargillo

brogue of Irish English can be traced in the speech patterns heard in Australia today. On the other hand, the variety contains many expressions which have originated in Australia (including a number from Aboriginal languages), and in recent years the influence of American English has been noticeable, so that the country now has a very mixed linguistic character.

In New Zealand (whose Maori name is *Aotearoa*), the story of English started later and moved more slowly. Captain Cook charted the islands in 1769–70, and European whalers and traders began to settle there in the 1790s, expanding the developments already taking place in Australia. Christian missionary work began among the Maori from about 1814. However, the official colony was not established until 1840, following the Treaty of Waitangi between Maori chiefs and the British Crown. There was then a rapid increase in European immigration – from around 2,000 in 1840 to 25,000 by 1850, and to three-quarters of a million by 1900. As early as the turn of the century visitors to the country were making comments on the emergence of a New Zealand accent. The total population in 1996 was over 3.5 million.

Three strands of New Zealand's social history in the present century have had especial linguistic consequences. Firstly, in comparison with Australia, there has been a stronger sense of the historical relationship with Britain, and a greater sympathy for British values and institutions. Many people speak with an accent which displays clear British influence. Secondly, there has been a growing sense of national identity, and in particular an emphasis on the differences between New Zealand and Australia. This has drawn attention to differences in the accents of the two countries, and motivated the use of distinctive New Zealand vocabulary. Thirdly, there has been a fresh concern to take account of the rights and needs of the Maori people, who now form over 10 per cent of the population. This has resulted in an increased use of Maori words in New Zealand English.

(*Opposite*) Map of Australia and New Zealand showing 1991 rounded population figures for states, territories and chief cities. Population totals are given in millions, e.g. 1.1 = 1,000,000; 0.08 = 80,000.

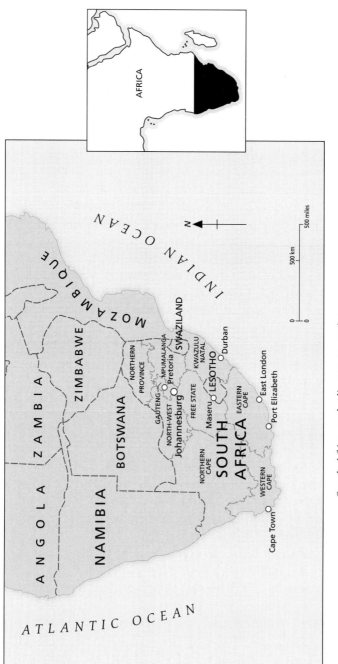

South Africa, and adjacent countries

South Africa

Although Dutch colonists arrived in the Cape as early as 1652, British involvement in the region dates only from 1795, during the Napoleonic Wars, when an expeditionary force invaded. British control was established in 1806, and a policy of settlement began in earnest in 1820, when some 5,000 British were given land in the eastern Cape. English was made the official language of the region in 1822, and there was an attempt to anglicize the large Afrikaans-speaking population. English became the language of law, education, and most other aspects of public life. Further British settlements followed in the 1840s and 1850s, especially in Natal, and there was a massive influx of Europeans following the development of the gold and diamond areas in the Witwatersrand in the 1870s. Nearly half a million immigrants, many of them English-speaking, arrived in the country during the last quarter of the nineteenth century.

The English language history of the region thus has many strands. There was initially a certain amount of regional dialect variation among the different groups of British settlers, with the speech of the London area prominent in the Cape, and Midlands and northern British speech strongly represented in Natal; but in due course a more homogeneous accent emerged – an accent that shares many similarities with the accents of Australia, which was also being settled during this period.

At the same time, English was being used as a second language by the Afrikaans speakers, and many of the Dutch colonists took this variety with them on the Great Trek of 1836, as they moved north to escape British rule. An African variety of English also developed, spoken by the black population, who had learned the language mainly in mission schools, and which was influenced in different ways by the various language backgrounds of the speakers. In addition, English came to be used, along with Afrikaans and often other languages, by those with an ethnically mixed background ('coloureds'); and it was also adopted by the many immigrants from India, who arrived in the country from around 1860.

English has always been a minority language in South Africa, and is currently spoken as a first language only by about 3.6 million in a 1996 population of nearly 42 million. Afrikaans, which was given official status in 1925, was the first language of the majority of whites, including most of those in power, and acted as an important symbol of identity for those of Afrikaner background. It was also the first language of most of the coloured population. English was used by the remaining whites (of British background) and by increasing numbers of the (70 per cent majority) black population. There is thus a linguistic side to the political divisions which have marked South African society in recent decades: Afrikaans came to be perceived by the black majority as the language of authority and repression; English was perceived by the white government as the language of protest and self-determination. Many blacks saw English as a means of achieving an international voice, and uniting themselves with other black communities.

On the other hand, the contemporary situation regarding the use of English is more complex than any simple opposition suggests. For the white authorities, too, English is important as a means of international communication, and 'upwardly mobile' Afrikaners have become increasingly bilingual, with fluent command of an English that often resembles the British-based variety. The public statements by South African politicians in recent years, seen on world television, illustrate this ability. As a result, a continuum of accents exists, ranging from those which are strongly influenced by Afrikaans to those which are very close to British Received Pronunciation. Such complexity is inevitable in a country where the overriding issue is social and political status, and where people have striven to maintain their deeply held feelings of national and ethnic identity in the face of opposition.

The 1993 Constitution names eleven languages as official, including English and Afrikaans, in an effort to enhance the status of the country's indigenous languages. The consequences of such an ambitious policy remain to be seen, but the difficulties of administering an eleven-language formula are immense (p. 81), and it is likely that English will continue to be an important lingua franca. Enthusiasm for the language continues to grow among the black population: in 1993, for example, a series of government surveys among black parents demonstrated an overwhelming choice of English as the preferred language in which children should receive their education. And in the South African Parliament in 1994 the language continued to dominate the proceedings, with 87 per cent of all speeches being made in English.

South Asia

In terms of numbers of English speakers, the Indian subcontinent ranks third in the world, after the USA and UK. This is largely due to the special position which the language has come to hold in India itself, where it has been estimated that some 4 or 5 per cent of the people now make regular use of English – approaching 40 million in 1996. There are also considerable numbers of English speakers elsewhere in the region, which comprises six countries (India, Bangladesh, Pakistan, Sri Lanka, Nepal, Bhutan) that together hold about a fifth of the world's population. Several varieties of English have emerged throughout the subcontinent, and they are sometimes collectively referred to as South Asian English. These varieties are less than 200 years old, but they are already among the most distinctive varieties in the English-speaking world.

The origins of South Asian English lie in Britain. The first regular British contact with the subcontinent came in 1600 with the formation of the British East India Company – a group of London merchants who were granted a trading monopoly in the area by Queen Elizabeth I. The Company established its first trading station at Surat in 1612, and by the end of the century others were in existence at Madras, Bombay and Calcutta. During the eighteeenth century, it overcame competition from other European nations, especially France. As the power of the Mughal emperors declined, the Company's influence grew, and in 1765 it took over the revenue management of Bengal. Following a period of financial indiscipline among Company servants, the 1784 India Act established a Board of Control responsible to the British Parliament, and in 1858, after the

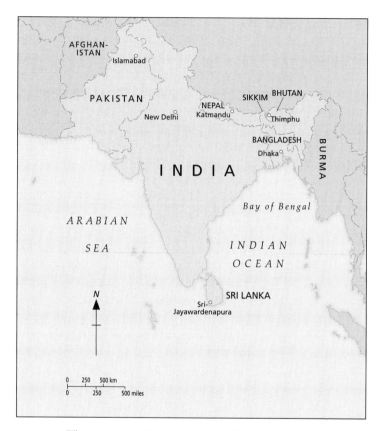

The countries where South Asian English is spoken

Indian Mutiny, the Company was abolished and its powers handed over to the Crown.

During the period of British sovereignty (the *Raj*), from 1765 until independence in 1947, English gradually became the medium of administration and education throughout the subcontinent. The language question attracted special attention during the early nineteenth century, when colonial administrators debated the kind of educational policy which should be introduced. A recognized turning-point was Lord William Bentinck's acceptance of a Minute written by Thomas Macaulay in 1835, which proposed the introduction of an English educational system in India. When the universities of Bombay, Calcutta and Madras were established in 1857, English became the primary medium of instruction, thereby guaranteeing its status and steady growth during the next century.

In India, the bitter conflict between the supporters of English, Hindi, and regional languages led in the 1960s to a 'three language formula', in which English was introduced as the chief alternative to the local state language (typically Hindi in the north and a regional language in the south). It now has the status of an 'associate' official language, with Hindi the official language. It is also recognized as the official language of four states (Manipur, Meghalaya, Nagaland, Tripura) and eight Union territories.

English has, as a consequence, retained its standing within Indian society, continuing to be used within the legal system, government administration, secondary and higher education, the armed forces, the media, business, and tourism. It is a strong unifying force. In the Dravidian-speaking areas of the south, it is widely preferred to Hindi as a lingua franca. In the north, its fortunes vary from state to state, in relation to Hindi, depending on the policies of those in power. In Pakistan, it is an associated official language. It has no official status in the other countries of South Asia, but throughout the region it is universally used as the medium of international communication.

Former colonial Africa

Despite several centuries of European trade with African nations, by the end of the eighteenth century only the Dutch at the Cape had established a permanent settlement. However, by 1914 colonial ambitions on the part of Britain, France, Germany, Portugal, Italy and Belgium had resulted in the whole continent (apart from Liberia and Ethiopia) being divided into colonial territories. After the two World Wars there was a repartitioning of the region, with the confiscation of German and Italian territories. Most of the countries created by this partition achieved independence in or after the 1960s, and the Organization of African Unity pledged itself to maintain existing boundaries.

The English began to visit West Africa from the end of the

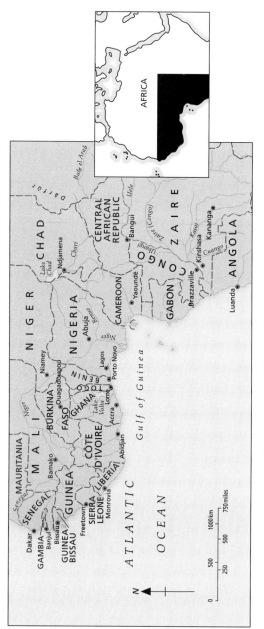

The countries of West Africa

fifteenth century, and soon after we find sporadic references to the use of the language as a lingua franca in some coastal settlements. By the beginning of the nineteenth century, the increase in commerce and anti-slave-trade activities had brought English to the whole West African coast. With hundreds of local languages to contend with, a particular feature of the region was the rise of several English-based pidgins and creoles, used alongside the standard varieties of colonial officials, missionaries, soldiers, and traders.

British varieties developed especially in five countries, each of which now gives English official status. There was also one American influence in the region.

- **Sierra Leone** In the 1780s, philanthropists in Britain bought land to establish a settlement for freed slaves, the first groups arriving from England, Nova Scotia and Jamaica. The settlement became a Crown Colony in 1808, and was then used as a base for anti-slave-trading squadrons, whose operations eventually brought some 60,000 'recaptives' to the country. The chief form of communication was an English-based creole, Krio, and this rapidly spread along the West African coast. The hinterland was declared a British protectorate in 1896; and the country received its independence in 1961. Its population had grown to over 4.6 million by 1996, most of whom can use Krio.
- **Ghana** (formerly **Gold Coast**) Following a successful British expedition against the Ashanti to protect trading interests, the southern Gold Coast was declared a Crown Colony in 1874. The modern state was created in 1957 by the union of this colony and the adjacent British Togoland trust territory, which had been mandated to Britain after World War I. Ghana was the first Commonwealth country to achieve independence, in 1960. Its population was over 16 million in 1996, about a million of whom use English as a second language.
- **Gambia** English trading along the Gambia River dates from the early seventeenth century. A period of conflict with France was followed in 1816 by the establishment of Bathurst

(modern Banjul) as a British base for anti-slaver activities. The capital became a Crown Colony in 1843, the country an independent member of the Commonwealth in 1965 and a republic in 1970. It had a population of just over a million in 1996. Krio is widely used as a lingua franca.

- **Nigeria** After a period of early nineteenth-century British exploration of the interior, a British colony was founded at Lagos in 1861. This amalgamated with other southern and northern territories to form a single country in 1914, and it received independence in 1960. Its population in 1996 was over 94 million. About half use pidgin or creole English as a second language.

- **Cameroon** Explored by the Portuguese, Spanish, Dutch and British, this region became a German protectorate in 1884, and was divided between France and Britain in 1919. After some uncertainty, the two areas merged as a single country in 1972, with both French and English remaining as official languages. It is a highly multilingual region, with a 1996 population of 13 million. It is thus a country in which contact languages have flourished, notably Cameroon Pidgin, spoken by about half the population.

- **Liberia** Africa's oldest republic was founded in 1822 through the activities of the American Colonization Society, which wished to establish a homeland for former slaves. Within fifty years it received some 13,000 black Americans, as well as some 6,000 slaves recaptured at sea. The settlement became a republic in 1847, and adopted a constitution based on that of the USA. It managed to retain its independence despite pressure from European countries during the nineteenth-century 'scramble for Africa'. Its population in 1996 was some 2.5 million, most of whom use pidgin English as a second language (but there are also a number of first-language speakers). Links with US African-American English are still very evident.

Although English ships had visited East Africa from the end of the sixteenth century, systematic interest began only in the 1850s, with the expeditions to the interior of such British explorers as Richard Burton, David Livingstone and John Speke. The Imperial British East Africa Company was founded in 1888, and soon afterwards a system of colonial protectorates became established, while other European nations (Germany, France, and Italy) vied with Britain for territorial control.

Five modern states, each with a history of British rule, gave English official status when they gained independence in the 1960s, and Zimbabwe followed suit in 1980. British English has thus played a major role in the development of these states, being widely used in government, the courts, schools, the media, and other public domains. It has also been adopted elsewhere in the region as a medium of international communication, such as in Ethiopia and Somalia.

- **Kenya** A British colony from 1920, this country became independent in 1963, following a decade of unrest (the Mau Mau rebellion). English was then made the official language, but Swahili replaced it in 1974. English none the less retains an important role in the country, which had some 28 million people in 1996.
- **Tanzania** (formerly **Zanzibar** and **Tanganyika**) Zanzibar became a British protectorate in 1890, and Britain received a mandate for Tanganyika in 1919. The first East African country to gain independence (1961), its population was over 27 million in 1996. English was a joint official language with Swahili until 1967, then lost its status. But it remains an important medium of communication.
- **Uganda** The Uganda kingdoms were united as a British protectorate between 1893 and 1903, and the country received its independence in 1962. Its population was over 18 million in 1996. English is the sole official language, but Swahili is also widely used as a lingua franca.
- **Malawi** (formerly **Nyasaland**) The area became a British colony in 1907, and received its independence in 1964. Its population was nearly 10 million in 1996. English is an official language along with Chewa.
- **Zambia** (formerly **Northern Rhodesia**) At first administered by the British South Africa Company, the country became a

The countries of East Africa

British protectorate in 1924, and received its independence in 1964. Its population was over 9 million in 1996. English is the official language.

- **Zimbabwe** (formerly **Southern Rhodesia**) Also administered by the British South Africa Company, it became a British colony in 1923. Opposition to independence under African rule led to a Unilateral Declaration of Independence (UDI) by the white-dominated government in 1965. Power was eventually transferred to the African majority, and the country achieved its independence in 1980. Its population was around 11 million in 1996. English is the official language.

The kinds of English which developed in East Africa were very different from those found in West Africa. Large numbers of British emigrants settled in the area, producing a class of expatriates and African-born whites (farmers, doctors, university lecturers, etc.) which never emerged in the environmentally less hospitable West African territories. A British model was introduced early on into schools, reinforcing the exposure to British English brought by the many missionary groups around the turn of the century. The result was a variety of mother-tongue English which has more in common with what is heard in South Africa or Australia than in Nigeria or Ghana.

South-east Asia and the South Pacific

The territories in and to the west of the South Pacific display an interesting mixture of American and British English. The main American presence emerged after the Spanish-American War of 1898, from which the USA received the island of Guam (and Puerto Rico in the Caribbean) and sovereignty over the Philippines. Hawaii was annexed at that time also, after a period of increasing US influence. In the 1940s, the US invasion of Japanese-held Pacific islands was followed after World War II by several areas being made the responsibility of the USA as United Nations Trust Territories. The Philippines became independent in 1946, but the influence of American English remains strong. And as this country has by far the largest population of the English-speaking states in the region (about 70 million in 1996), it makes a significant contribution to world totals.

British influence began through the voyages of English sailors at the end of the eighteenth century, notably the journeys of Captain Cook in the 1770s. The London Missionary Society sent its workers to the islands of the South Pacific fifty years later. In

South-east Asia, the development of a British colonial empire grew from the work of Stamford Raffles, an administrator in the British East India Company. Centres were established in several locations, notably Penang (1786), Singapore (1819) and Malacca (1824). Within a few months, the population of Singapore had grown to over 5,000, and by the time the Federated Malay States were brought together as a Crown Colony (1867), English had come to be established throughout the region as the medium of law and administration, and was being increasingly used in other contexts. A famous example is the English-language daily newspaper, *The Straits Times*, which began publication in 1845.

English inevitably and rapidly became the language of power in the British territories of South-east Asia. Hong Kong island was ceded to Britain in 1842 by the Treaty of Nanking, at the end of the first Opium War, and Kowloon was added to it in 1860; the New Territories, which form the largest part of the colony, were leased from China in 1898 for ninety-nine years. Towards the end of the nineteenth century, several territories in the region became British protectorates, the administration of some being later taken over by Australia and New Zealand.

The introduction of a British educational system exposed learners to a standard British English model very early on. English-medium schools began in Penang (now Malaysia's leading port) in 1816, with senior teaching staff routinely brought in from Britain. Although at the outset these schools were attended by only a tiny percentage of the population, numbers increased during the nineteenth century as waves of Chinese and Indian immigrants entered the area. English rapidly became the language of professional advancement and the chief literary language. Soon after the turn of the century, higher education through the medium of English was also introduced. The language thus became a prestige lingua franca among those who had received an English education and who had thereby entered professional society.

Despite the common colonial history of the region, a single variety of 'South-east Asian English' has not emerged. The political histories of Singapore and Malaysia, especially since independence, have been too divergent for this to happen; and the sociolinguistic situations in Hong Kong and Papua New Guinea are unique.

- **Singapore** In the 1950s a bilingual educational system was introduced in Singapore, with English used as a unifying medium alongside Chinese, Malay, or Tamil. However, English remained the language of government and the legal system, and retained its importance in education and the media. Its use has also been steadily increasing among the general population. In a 1975 survey, only 27 per cent of people over age forty claimed to understand English, whereas among fifteen- to twenty-year-olds, the proportion was over 87 per cent. There is also evidence of quite widespread use in family settings. The country had a population of around 3 million in 1996.
- **Malaysia** The situation is very different in Malaysia where, following independence (1957), Bahasa Malaysia was adopted as the national language, and the role of English accordingly became more restricted. Malay-medium education was introduced, with English an obligatory subject but increasingly being seen as of value for international rather than intranational purposes – more a foreign language than a second language. However, the traditional prestige attached to English still exists, for many speakers. The country had a population of over 20 million in 1996.
- **Hong Kong** English has always had a limited use in the territory, associated with government or military administration, law, business, and the media. Chinese (Cantonese) is the mother-tongue of over 98 per cent of the population (around 6 million in 1996). However, in recent years there has been a major increase in educational provision, with 1992 estimates suggesting that over a quarter of the population now have some competence in English. English and Chinese have joint official status, but Chinese predominates in most speech situations, often with a great deal of language mixing. There is considerable uncertainty surrounding the future role of English, after the 1997 transfer of power.

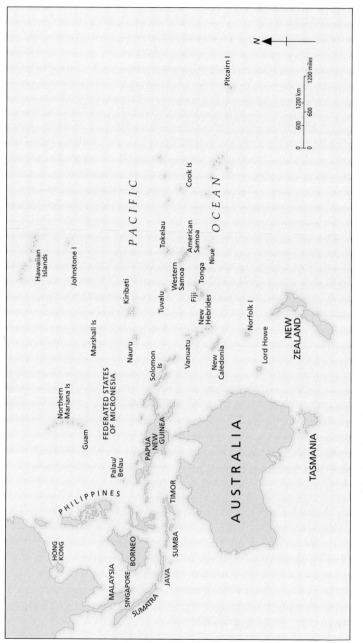

The location of territories in South-east Asia and the South Pacific

- **Papua New Guinea** British sailors visited the territory as early as 1793. It became a British protectorate in 1884, was mandated to Australia in 1920, and became independent in 1975. There was a population of nearly 4.5 million in 1996. About half the people speak Tok Pisin, an English-based pidgin, as a second language (and some have it as a mother tongue). It has a nation-wide presence, widely seen in advertisements and the press, and heard on radio and television. Many major works have been translated into Tok Pisin, including Shakespeare and the Bible.

A world view

The present-day world status of English is primarily the result of two factors: the expansion of British colonial power, which peaked towards the end of the nineteenth century, and the emergence of the United States as the leading economic power of the twentieth century. It is the latter factor which continues to explain the world position of the English language today (much to the discomfiture of some in Britain who find the loss of historical linguistic pre-eminence unpalatable). The USA has nearly 70 per cent of all English mother-tongue speakers in the world (excluding creole varieties). Such dominance, with its political and economic underpinnings, currently gives the Americans a controlling interest in the way the language is likely to develop.

How then may we summarize this complex situation? The US linguist Braj Kachru has suggested that we think of the spread of English around the world as three concentric circles, representing different ways in which the language has been acquired and is currently used. Although not all countries fit neatly into this model, it has been widely regarded as a helpful approach to classification.

- The *inner circle* refers to the traditional bases of English, where it is the primary language: it includes the USA, UK, Ireland, Canada, Australia and New Zealand.
- The *outer* or *extended circle* involves the earlier phases of the

53

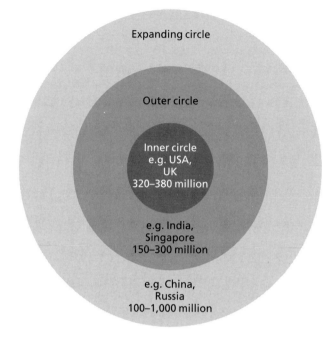

The three 'circles' of English

spread of English in non-native settings, where the language has become part of a country's chief institutions, and plays an important 'second language' role in a multilingual setting: it includes Singapore, India, Malawi and over fifty other territories.

- The *expanding circle* involves those nations which recognize the importance of English as an international language, though they do not have a history of colonization by members of the inner circle, nor have they given English any special administrative status. It includes China, Japan, Greece, Poland and (as the name of this circle suggests) a steadily increasing number of other states. In these areas, English is taught as a foreign language.

There are some seventy-five territories in which English has held or continues to hold a special place, as a member of either the inner or the outer circles. These are given in a single alphabetical list below, along with an estimate of the number of speakers. The national population figures are estimates for mid-1995. L1 stands for people who have a variety of English as a first language, or mother tongue. L2 stands for people who have learned a variety of English as a second language, in addition to their mother tongue. Where I have been unable to find any relevant data, the figure for L1 or L2 is missing. Lists of this kind contain all kinds of hidden assumptions, and they have to be carefully interpreted. In particular, we should note the following points:

- There is no single source of statistical information on language totals, so estimates have to be taken from a variety of sources. In the first instance, I used the *UNESCO Statistical Yearbook* (1995), the *Encyclopedia Britannica Yearbook* (1996), the 12th edition of *Ethnologue: Languages of the World* (1992), and whatever census data I could find. In a (regrettably) few cases, a sociolinguistic study of an area has provided an estimate.
- Where no linguistic estimate is available (the cases are marked with an asterisk), I have used an indirect method, based on the percentage of a country's population over the age of twenty-five who have completed their secondary or further education – the assumption being that, in a country where the language has official status, and is taught in schools, this figure would suggest a reasonable level of attainment.
- The notion of 'a variety of English' referred to above includes standard, pidgin, and creole varieties of English. That is why, in certain countries, the usage totals in the list are much higher than would be expected if only standard English were being considered. In Nigeria, for example, large numbers (thought to be well over 40 per cent of the population) use Nigerian Pidgin English as a second language. The linguistic justification for this approach is that these varieties are, indeed, varieties **of English** (as opposed to, say, French), and are usually related to standard English along a continuum. On the other hand, because the ends of this continuum may not be

mutually intelligible, it could be argued that we need to keep standard English totals separate from pidgin/creole English totals: if this view is adopted, then some 5–6 million L1 speakers and some 50–60 million L2 speakers should be subtracted from the grand totals below. Countries where this is an issue are identified by (c) in the list.

- It is also important to recall (from chapter 1) that to have a 'special place' can mean various things. Sometimes English is an official or joint official language of a state, its status being defined by law, as in the case of India, Ireland or Canada. Sometimes it may be the sole or dominant language for historical reasons, as in the case of the USA or the UK. In a few instances, such as Kenya and Tanzania, English has lost the formal status it once had, though it still plays an important role in the community. In many cases, its standing is less certain, coexisting with other local languages in a relationship which shifts with time and social function. But in all cases, it can be argued, the population is living in an environment in which the English language is routinely in evidence, publicly accessible in varying degrees, and part of the nation's recent or present identity.

- Finally, we should bear in mind that the notion of a 'special place', as reflected in this list, is one which relates entirely to historical and political factors. This has led some linguists to argue that such a list presents a picture of the present-day world which does not wholly reflect sociolinguistic reality. In particular, it is suggested, the distinction between 'second language' (L2) and 'foreign language' use has less contemporary relevance than it formerly had. There is much more use of English nowadays in some countries of the expanding circle, where it is 'only' a foreign language (as in Scandinavia and The Netherlands), than in some of the outer circle where it has traditionally held a special place. To make a language official may not mean very much, in real terms. For example, English is probably represented in Rwanda and Burundi in very comparable ways, but Rwanda is in the list (and Burundi is not) only because the former has (in 1996) made a political decision to give the language special status. What the consequences are for the future use of English in that country remains to be seen. In the meantime, it should not be forgotten that there are several countries, not represented below, which are making a much more important contribution to the notion of English as a global language than is reflected by any geo-historical picture (see chapters 3 and 4).

Territory	Population (1995)	Usage estimate	
American Samoa	58,000	L1	2,000
		L2	56,000
Antigua & Barbuda (c)	64,000	L1	61,000
		L2	2,000
Australia	18,025,000	L1	15,316,000
		L2	2,084,000
Bahamas (c)	276,000	L1	250,000
		L2	25,000
Bangladesh	120,093,000	L2	3,100,000
Barbados (c)	265,000	L1	265,000
Belize (c)	216,000	L1	135,000
		L2	30,000
Bermuda	61,000	L1	60,000
Bhutan	1,200,000	L2	60,000
Botswana	1,549,000	L2	620,000
British Virgin Islands (c)	18,000	L1	17,000
Brunei	291,000	L1	10,000
		L2	104,000*
Cameroon (c)	13,233,000	L2	6,600,000
Canada	29,463,000	L1	19,700,000
		L2	6,000,000
Cayman Islands	29,000	L1	29,000
Cook Islands	19,000	L1	1,000
		L2	2,000
Dominica	72,000	L1	3,000
		L2	12,000*
Fiji	791,000	L1	5,000
		L2	160,000
Gambia (c)	1,115,000	L2	33,000*
Ghana (c)	16,472,000	L2	1,153,000*

Territory	Population (1995)	Usage estimate	
Gibraltar	28,000	L1	25,000
		L2	2,000
Grenada (c)	92,000	L1	91,000
Guam	149,000	L1	56,000
		L2	92,000
Guyana (c)	770,000	L1	700,000
		L2	30,000
Hong Kong	6,205,000	L1	125,000
		L2	1,860,000
India	935,744,000	L1	320,000
		L2	37,000,000
Ireland	3,590,000	L1	3,400,000
		L2	190,000
Jamaica (c)	2,520,000	L1	2,400,000
		L2	50,000
Kenya	28,626,000	L2	2,576,000*
Kiribati	80,000	L2	20,000*
Lesotho	2,050,000	L2	488,000*
Liberia (c)	2,380,000	L1	60,000
		L2	2,000,000
Malawi	9,939,000	L2	517,000*
Malaysia	19,948,000	L1	375,000
		L2	5,984,000
Malta	370,000	L1	8,000
		L2	86,000*
Marshall Islands	56,000	L2	28,000*
Mauritius	1,128,000	L1	2,000
		L2	167,000*
Micronesia	105,000	L1	4,000
		L2	15,000*
Montserrat (c)	11,000	L1	11,000
Namibia	1,651,000	L1	13,000
		L2	300,000*
Nauru	10,000	L1	800
		L2	9,400
Nepal	20,093,000	L2	5,927,000*
New Zealand	3,568,000	L1	3,396,000
		L2	150,000

Territory	Population (1995)	Usage estimate	
Nigeria (c)	95,434,000	L2	43,000,000
Northern Marianas (c)	58,000	L1	3,000
		L2	50,000
Pakistan	140,497,000	L2	16,000,000
Palau	17,000	L1	500
		L2	16,300
Papua New Guinea (c)	4,302,000	L1	120,000
		L2	2,800,000
Philippines	70,011,000	L1	15,000
		L2	36,400,000
Puerto Rico	3,725,000	L1	110,000
		L2	1,746,000
Rwanda	7,855,000	L2	24,000*
St Kitts & Nevis (c)	39,000	L1	39,000
St Lucia (c)	143,000	L1	29,000
		L2	22,000
St Vincent & Grenadines (c)	112,000	L1	111,000
Seychelles	75,000	L1	2,000
		L2	11,000*
Sierra Leone (c)	4,509,000	L1	450,000
		L2	3,830,000
Singapore	2,989,000	L1	300,000
		L2	1,046,000
Solomon Islands (c)	382,000	L1	2,000
		L2	135,000
South Africa	41,465,000	L1	3,600,000
		L2	10,000,000*
Sri Lanka	18,090,000	L1	10,000
		L2	1,850,000
Suriname (c)	430,000	L1	258,000
		L2	150,000
Swaziland	913,000	L2	40,000*
Tanzania	28,072,000	L2	3,000,000
Tonga	100,000	L2	30,000*
Trinidad & Tobago (c)	1,265,000	L1	1,200,000
Tuvalu	9,000	L2	600
Uganda	18,659,000	L2	2,000,000*

Territory	Population (1995)	Usage estimate	
United Kingdom	58,586,000	L1	56,990,000
		L2	1,100,000
UK Islands (Channel Is, Man)	218,000	L1	217,000
United States	263,057,000	L1	226,710,000
		L2	30,000,000
US Virgin Islands (c)	98,000	L1	79,000
		L2	10,000
Vanuatu (c)	168,000	L1	2,000
		L2	160,000
Western Samoa	166,000	L1	1,000
		L2	86,000
Zambia	9,456,000	L1	50,000
		L2	1,000,000*
Zimbabwe	11,261,000	L1	250,000
		L2	3,300,000*
Other dependencies	30,000	L1	18,000
		L2	12,000
Total	2,024,614,000	L1	337,407,300
		L2	235,351,300

The category 'Other dependencies' consists of territories administered by Australia (Norfolk I., Christmas I., Cocos Is), New Zealand (Niue, Tokelau) and the UK (Anguilla, Falkland Is, Pitcairn I., Turks & Caicos Is).

In reflecting on these totals, we should not underestimate the significance of the overall population figure, as it indicates the total number of people who are in theory routinely exposed to English in a country. The grand total of 2,025 million in 1995 is equivalent in 1997 (assuming a world population rate of increase of 1.6 per cent per annum) to 2,090 million, which is well over a third of the world's population. But of course, only a proportion of these people actually have some command of English.

The total of 337 million represents an estimate of those who have learned English as a first language (L1). The total would be increased if we knew the L1 figures for every country – especially in such areas as West Africa, where it is not known how many use a variety of English as a first language – and some reference books (such as *World Almanac* and *Ethnologue*) do cite as many as 450 million as a grand total at present.

The total of 235 million represents an estimate of those who have learned English as a second language (L2); but it does not give the whole picture. For many countries, no estimates are available. And in others (notably India, Pakistan, Nigeria, Ghana, Malaysia, Philippines and Tanzania, which had a combined total of over 1,300 million people in 1995), even a small percentage increase in the number of speakers thought to have a reasonable (rather than a fluent) command of English would considerably expand the L2 grand total. A figure of 350 million is in fact widely cited as a likely total for this category.

No account has been taken in this list of the third category of English language learners referred to above: the members of the expanding circle, who have learned English as a foreign language. Estimates for the total number of these speakers vary enormously: they have been as low as 100 million and as high as 1,000 million. Here too, everything depends on just how great a command of English is considered acceptable to count as a 'speaker of English'. One thing is plain: as we shall see in chapter 4, their role in any account of the global English picture is likely to increase dramatically in the twenty-first century, eventually exceeding the significance currently attached to the outer-circle countries. Numerically, much will depend on what happens in the countries with the largest populations, notably China, Japan, Russia, Indonesia and Brazil.

If we are cautious by temperament, we will add these statistics together by choosing the lowest estimates in each category: in this way we shall end up with a grand total of 670 million people with a native or native-like command of English. If we go to the opposite extreme, and use a criterion of 'reasonable competence' rather than 'native-like fluency', we shall end up with a grand total of 1,800 million. A 'middle-of-the-road' estimate would be 1,200–1,500 million, and this is now commonly encountered.

No other language has spread around the globe so extensively, but – as we have seen in chapter 1 – what is impressive is not so much the grand total but the speed with which expansion has

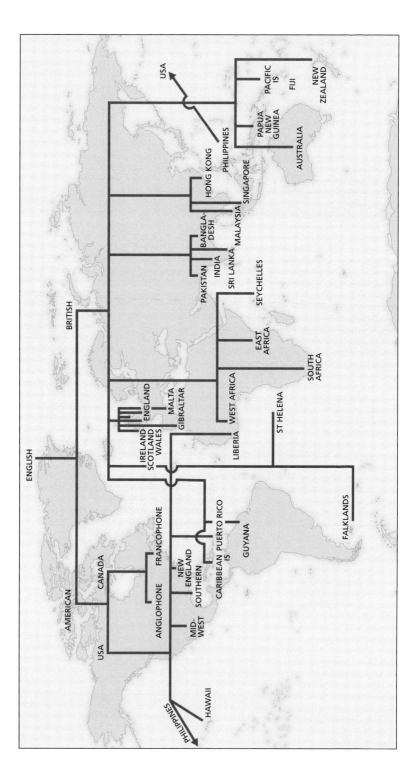

ENGLISH

ENGLISH

AMERICAN

BRITISH

USA

CANADA

ANGLOPHONE

FRANCOPHONE

MID-WEST

NEW ENGLAND

SOUTHERN

CARIBBEAN IS

PUERTO RICO

GUYANA

HAWAII

PHILIPPINES

IRELAND

SCOTLAND

WALES

ENGLAND

MALTA

GIBRALTAR

WEST AFRICA

LIBERIA

ST HELENA

FALKLANDS

SOUTH AFRICA

EAST AFRICA

SEYCHELLES

PAKISTAN

INDIA

SRI LANKA

BANGLA-DESH

MALAYSIA

SINGAPORE

HONG KONG

PHILIPPINES

USA

PAPUA NEW GUINEA

AUSTRALIA

PACIFIC IS

FIJI

NEW ZEALAND

taken place since the 1950s. In 1950, the case for English as a world language would have been no more than plausible. Fifty years on, and the case is virtually unassailable. What happened in this fifty years – a mere eye-blink in the history of a language – to cause such a massive change of stature? To answer this question, we must look at the way modern society has come to use, and depend on, the English language.

(*Opposite*) A family tree representation of the way English has spread around the world, showing the influence of the two main branches of American and British English

3

Why English?
The cultural foundation

'I have undertaken to write a grammar of English', says John Wallis in the preface to his *Grammar of the English Language*, 'because there is clearly a great demand for it from foreigners, who want to be able to understand the various important works which are written in our tongue.' And he goes on: 'all kinds of literature are widely available in English editions, and, without boasting, it can be said that there is scarcely any worthwhile body of knowledge which has not been recorded today, adequately at least, in the English language'.

This is a familiar-sounding argument, to twentieth-century ears; but these bold words are not from a modern author. John Wallis was writing in England in 1765. Moreover, the words are a translation. Wallis wrote his book in Latin, which was still being widely used as a scholarly lingua franca during the eighteenth century. But he could clearly see how the situation was changing – and had already greatly changed since the time of Shakespeare.

A few generations earlier, Richard Mulcaster, the headmaster of Merchant Taylors' School, had been one of the strongest supporters of the English language, avowing in 1582: 'I love Rome, but London better. I favour Italy, but England more. I honour the Latin, but I worship the English.' However, Mulcaster was living in a very different intellectual climate. He felt he had to defend the language against those who believed that

English should not usurp the long-established place of Latin. There were many around him who thought that a 'mere vernacular' could not be used to express great and complex thoughts. So he expressed himself strongly: 'I do not think that any language is better able to utter all arguments, either with more pith or greater plainness, as our English tongue is'. A decade later, and Shakespeare would begin to prove him right.

Despite his strong convictions, Mulcaster could still see that there was a problem: English was no real match for Latin at an international level. 'Our English tongue', he says at one point, 'is of small reach – it stretcheth no further than this island of ours – nay, not there over all.' He was right, for the Celtic languages were still strongly present in Britain at the time, and few people engaged in foreign travel. 'Our state', Mulcaster remarks, 'is no Empire to hope to enlarge it by commanding over countries.' But within two years, Walter Raleigh's first expedition to America had set sail, and the situation was about to alter fundamentally.

Not all were as pessimistic as Mulcaster, though. Samuel Daniel, in his poem *Musophilis*, wrote in 1599:

> And who in time knows whither we may vent
>   The treasure of our tongue, to what strange shores
> This gain of our best glory shall be sent,
> To enrich unknowing nations without stores?
> Which worlds in the yet unformed Occident
> May come refined with the accents that are ours.

Daniel's speculations did become a reality – but not for well over a century. When, fifty years later, the poet and traveller Richard Flecknoe reflected on his ten-year journey through Europe, Asia, Africa and America he found that Spanish and Dutch were the really useful languages to know, with English being only occasionally helpful – as he put it, 'to stop holes with'. But by the 1750s it was possible for the Earl of Chesterfield to write: 'I have . . . a sensible pleasure in reflecting upon the rapid progress which our language has lately made, and still continues to make, all over Europe.' And David Hume, writing in 1767 at a time when French was recognized as the language of international diplomacy, saw in America the key to the future success of English: 'Let the French, therefore, triumph in the present diffusion of their tongue. Our solid and increasing establishments in America . . . promise a superior stability and duration to the English language'.

Many Americans agreed. In 1780 John Adams, as part of his proposal to Congress for an American Academy, was in no doubt. 'English is destined to be in the next and succeeding centuries more generally the language of the world than Latin was in the last or French is in the present age. The reason of this is obvious, because the increasing population in America, and their universal connection and correspondence with all nations will, aided by the influence of England in the world, whether great or small, force their language into general use, in spite of all the obstacles that may be thrown in their way, if any such there should be'. He proved to be an accurate prophet.

We might expect that the British and Americans would themselves be loud in support of their own language. Indeed, often their views were expressed with an extravagance that we would now find embarrassing, claiming even to see divine providence in the spread of English, or suggesting that there was something intrinsically superior about its pronunciation or grammatical construction – a view which I rejected in chapter 1. It was therefore a moment of some significance when in 1851 a German, Jakob Grimm, the leading philologist of his time, commented that 'of all modern languages, not one has acquired such great strength and vigour as the English', and concluded that it 'may be called justly a language of the world . . . destined to reign in future with still more extensive sway over all parts of the globe'.

His view was much quoted, and during the nineteenth century similar opinions multiplied as British imperialism grew. US linguist Richard W. Bailey, in his cultural history of the language, *Images of English* (1991), has compiled a number of comments from contemporary writers which show just how the mood had changed by the 1850s. One quotation will suffice to illustrate the prevailing opinion – from a writer to *Gentleman's Magazine* in February 1829:

It is evident to all those who have devoted any portion of attention to the subject, that the English language would, if proper care were devoted to its advancement, stand an excellent chance of becoming more universally diffused, read, and spoken, than any other now is, or ever has been. In Europe, the study of it seems to be gradually spreading. In Germany, Russia, and Scandinavia it is esteemed an essential, in France a highly useful, branch of education; in Africa it is gradually superseding the Dutch, and becoming the medium of valuable information. In Australasia it is not only widely spoken, as the only European language known on that vast continent, but written and printed in an almost incredible number of newspapers, magazines, and reviews. In Asia so great is the desire manifested to learn it, that it was thought by Bishop Heber, that, if proper facilities were afforded, it would, in fifty years, supersede Hindoostanee, and become the court and camp language of India. In America, millions already speak, write, and read it, as their mother tongue . . . Never before did a language look forward to so bright a prospect as this . . .

And indeed, by the end of the century, as we have seen in chapter 1, English had become the language 'on which the sun never sets'.

Then, as today, some enthusiasts were moved to speculate about the world's linguistic future in ways which can best be described as fantasy. About 60 million people were speaking English around the world as a mother tongue by the 1850s – a remarkable increase indeed – but this led many writers to become very excited about the language's prospects. By the turn of the century, some calculated, there would surely be at least three times as many. And, others were predicting in the 1870s, after a further century the grand total of mother-tongue speakers would almost certainly reach a 1,000 million – at least! Here is the editor of *The Phonetic Journal* (Isaac Pitman), writing in the issue of 13 September 1873 about the future of English. He observes that the contemporary users of English number nearly 80 million, then uses formulae on population projections in various countries to reach the following conclusion:

We may estimate on this basis that in the year 2000 the most important languages will be spoken by the number of persons as under:

Italian		53,370,000
French		72,571,000
Russian		130,479,800
German		157,480,000
Spanish		505,286,242
English		
Europe	178,846,153	⎫
United States and non-European		⎬ 1,837,286,53
British dependencies	1,658,440,000	⎭

Such predictions were very wide of the mark, as we have seen in chapter 2. Even the most optimistic of estimates for mother-tongue usage in the 1990s hardly exceeds 450 million. The late nineteenth-century writers were making assumptions which were soon to prove false – that empire-building would continue at the same rate, that British industrial supremacy would be maintained, and that those who spoke minority languages would not fight back. Predicting the linguistic future is always a dangerous activity.

But the general thrust of their argument was certainly borne out, and if we include second and foreign language usage of English in the 1990s, then the prophets were more right than wrong. 'English is the language of the future', wrote William White in the weekly *The Schoolmaster* in 1872, and Pitman concludes his calculations with exactly the same words. These are two out of hundreds of quotations it is possible to find in the literature of the time making this point. I have not found a single quotation to suggest that a different view was held by anyone.

These observations reinforce the historical account given in chapter 2, illustrating the remarkably short period of time it took for English to travel around the world. But they do not give the whole story. After all, when a language arrives in a new country, it does not necessarily come to be adopted. It has to prove its worth. And there are famous occasions where the language of the newcomers does *not* end up replacing the language of the inhabitants – the most famous instance, in fact, relating to English itself, in 1066. Within 200 years of the Norman Conquest, the language of England was emerging, in the earliest Middle English literature, as – English, not French. There was no linguistic conquest. Perhaps, if the Normans had taken up residence in larger numbers, or if good political relations between England and France had lasted longer, or if English had not already been so well established since Anglo-Saxon times, the outcome might have been different. This book would then, in all probability, have been written about (and in) World French.

So what was the worth of the English language, as it grew in global stature during the nineteenth century? In which ways did people value it? In which ways have they since come to use it? In which situations do they now depend on it? The answers to these questions will give us a sense of the language's social usefulness, which is actually more informative, in addressing the question 'Why World English?' than any bare historical account of the language's geographical spread (such as the one provided in chapter 2). A geo-historical survey can help us see what happened in the past; but a socio-historical account is needed to help us explain it; and only a cultural account can give us a sense of what is likely to happen in the future.

The remainder of this chapter therefore reviews some important factors in nineteenth-century social history which laid the cultural foundation for the eventual growth of English as a world language. Then in chapter 4 we shall examine the various cultural manifestations of this development during the twentieth century which will explain the stature of the language today. We shall encounter a series of variations on a single theme. In relation to so many of the major socio-cultural developments of the past 200 years, it can be shown that the English language has repeatedly found itself 'in the right place at the right time'. No single one of these developments could have established the language as a world leader, but together they have put it in a position of pre-eminence, and together they maintain it.

Political developments

Most of the pre-twentieth-century commentators would have had no difficulty giving a single, political answer to the question 'Why World English?' They would simply have pointed to the growth of the British Empire. Isaac Pitman, for example, justifying his 1873 calculations about English as the language of the future (see p. 67), simply observes: 'The British Empire covers nearly a third of the earth's surface, and British subjects are nearly a fourth of the population of the world.' It was considered self-evident that the civilizing influence of Britain was a desirable goal, anywhere in the world, and that the English language was an essential means of achieving this end. (Similar opinions were of course being expressed by other cultures too, notably the French.)

The strength of feeling on this point has to be appreciated, for it helps to explain the intensity with which the language came to be introduced in many countries, during the period of Empire, and the resources which were poured into it to guarantee the success of its new role. Here is William Russel, writing in 1801:

if many schools were established in different parts of Asia and Africa to instruct the natives, free of all expense, with various premiums [prizes] of British manufacture to the most meritorious pupils, this would be the best preparatory step that Englishmen could adopt for the general admission of their commerce, their opinions, their religion. This would tend to conquer the heart and its affections; which is a far more effectual conquest than that obtained by swords and cannons: and a thousand pounds expended for tutors, books, and premiums would do more to subdue a nation of savages than forty thousand expended for artillery-men, bullets, and gunpowder.

The triumphalist attitude is unpalatable today, but it well illustrates the mood of the time. William White is even more explicit about the role the English language can play, when it is introduced into a new part of the world. Talking in 1872 about the many languages of India, he comments:

As we link Calcutta with Bombay, and Bombay with Madras, and by roads, railways, and telegraphs interlace province with province, we may in process of time fuse India into unity, and the use and prevalence of our language may be the register of the progress of that unity.

The register of the progress of that unity. That is the vision which is repeatedly encountered as we trace the path of English around the British Empire: the language as a guarantor, as well as a symbol, of political unity. It is a vision, moreover, which continued to prove compelling a century later, when the evidence of that Empire was rapidly vanishing from the atlas. Many of the newly independent multilingual countries, especially in Africa, chose English as their official language to enable speakers of their indigenous communities to continue communicating with each other at a national level. And the concept of language as a political symbol still emerges every time people perceive the unity of their country to be threatened by minority movements – as we shall see in chapter 5, in relation to English in present-day USA.

In the context of colonialism, the desire for national linguistic unity is the other side of the coin from the desire for international linguistic unity. The language of a colonial power introduces a new, unifying medium of communication within a colony, but at the same time it reflects the bonds between that colony and the home country. In the case of English, these bonds were of especial significance, because of the special nature of the historical period during which they were being formed. They brought immediate access to a culture which more than any other had been responsible for the Industrial Revolution.

Access to knowledge

As we saw in chapter 1, by the beginning of the nineteenth century, Britain had become the world's leading industrial and trading nation. Its population of 5 million in 1700 more than doubled by 1800, and during that century no country could equal its economic growth, with a gross national product rising, on average, at 2 per cent a year. Most of the innovations of the Industrial Revolution were of British origin: the harnessing of coal, water and steam to drive heavy machinery; the development of new materials, techniques and equipment in a wide range of manufacturing industries; and the emergence of new means of transportation. By 1800, the chief growth areas, in textiles and mining, were producing a range of manufactured goods for export which led to Britain being called the 'workshop of the world'. Names such as Thomas Newcomen, James Watt, Matthew Boulton, Richard Trevithick, George Stephenson,

Charles Wheatstone, Michael Faraday, Humphry Davy, Thomas Telford and Henry Bessemer reflect the British achievement of that time.

The linguistic consequences of this achievement were far-reaching. The new terminology of technological and scientific advance had an immediate impact on the language, adding tens of thousands of words to the English lexicon. But, more important, the fact that these innovations were pouring out of an English-speaking country meant that those from abroad who wished to learn about them would need to learn English – and learn it well – if they wished to benefit. Especially after the French Wars (1792–1815), missions of inquiry arrived in Britain from several continental countries, foreign workers were seconded to British factories, and many Britons came to earn a good living abroad, teaching the new methods of industrial production.

The magnet of opportunity in Britain attracted several inventors from the Continent, who subsequently became leaders in their field. Here are three famous instances, from the beginning, the middle, and the end of the nineteenth century. The civil engineer Marc Isambard Brunel was born in France, but fled the Revolution to the USA, before moving to England in 1799. William Siemens, the steel manufacturer, was born in Prussia, but settled in London in the 1840s. And Gugliemo Marconi was born in Italy (though his mother was Irish), but received little encouragement there for his experiments, and from 1896 worked in London, where he filed his first patent.

It was not long before similar developments were taking place in America which, by the end of the century, had overtaken Britain as the world's fastest growing economy. There is a corresponding litany of US inventors who maintained the momentum of the Industrial Revolution in Europe and began to rival their European counterparts in fame, as such names as Benjamin Franklin, Thomas Edison, Samuel Morse and Robert Fulton suggest. Gradually, America in turn acted as a magnet for European scholars, such as glaciologist Jean-Louis Agassiz (in 1846), electrical engineer Nikola Tesla (in 1884), and industrial chemist Leo Baekeland (in 1889). When the American research is added to the British, it is possible to suggest that about half of the influential scientific and technological output in the period between 1750 to 1900 would have been written in English. If we analyse the entries in the *Chambers Concise Dictionary of Scientists* (a book which has been praised for its attention to internationalism), we find that 45 per cent of the people from this period were working routinely in an English-language environment, and several more were collaborating with English-speaking scholars.

The nature of the Industrial Revolution would have been very different if it had not been supported by developments which made the new knowledge widely available. Indeed, some of the technology was itself critical in helping the dissemination of ideas. In particular, steam technology revolutionized printing, enabling the introduction of the high-speed rotary press and the Linotype machine for casting and setting type, and generating an unprecedented mass of publications in English – technical manuals and leaflets, books of instructions, specialized and popular periodicals, advertisements, and proceedings of learned societies. And as the innovations made their impact on America, the amount of expository material in the English language increased dramatically.

Access to the new knowledge was also much helped by progress in transportation. During the first half of the nineteenth century, the growth of new transport systems, especially the steamship and the railway, began the process of bringing people closer together. During the second half, the growth of new communication systems, especially the telegraph and telephone, made contact between people virtually instantaneous. In 1815, it took four days for news of the Battle of Waterloo to reach London. In 1915, news from the Gallipoli campaign in the Dardanelles was arriving by the hour.

Increasingly rapid and robust methods of transportation transformed the availability of the products of the Industrial Revolution. New methods of mass production demanded new means of mass transportation. In particular, as far as the language was concerned, the distribution of daily newspapers on a large scale would not have been possible without a railway system and, later, a road network capable of carrying increasingly heavy vehicles. Another major step was the arrival of new sources of energy. Edwin L. Drake bored the first oil well in Pennsylvania in 1859, and by 1880 the Standard Oil Company, under John D. Rockefeller and his associates, was controlling the refining of over 90 per cent of all oil produced in the USA.

Standard Oil was but one of several giant organizations to emerge in the USA during the later decades of the century, nurtured by the huge natural resources of the country and the demands of its rapidly growing population. Another was the newspaper empire of William Randolph Hearst. A third was the manufacturing, banking, and transportation empire of financier John Pierpont Morgan. By the turn of the century his banking house had become one of the world's most powerful financial institutions, helping to finance the supply and credit needs of the Allies in the First World War, and much of the cost of post-war European reconstruction. The only country to have developed comparable financial and industrial strengths, during the last quarter of the nineteenth century, was Germany; but these were to disappear following defeat in 1918, leaving the ground clear for American economic domination.

The early nineteenth century had seen the rapid growth of the international banking system, especially in Germany, Britain, and the USA. The new organizations supported the fortunes of the developing industrial companies, handled government securities, and facilitated the growth of world trade and investment. In particular, the less wealthy countries of Europe, as well as the new colonies further afield, urgently needed to attract foreign investment. Firms such as Rothschilds and Morgans grew in response to these needs, and London and New York became the investment capitals of the world.

In 1914, Britain and the USA were together investing over £4,500 thousand million abroad – three times as much as France and almost four times as much as Germany. The resulting 'economic imperialism' brought a fresh dimension to the balance of linguistic power. 'Access to knowledge' now became 'access to knowledge about how to get financial backing'. If the metaphor 'money talks' has any meaning at all, those were the days when it was shouting loudly – and the language in which it was shouting was chiefly English.

Taken for granted

The story of English throughout this period is one of rapid expansion and diversification, with innovation after innovation coming to use the language as a primary or sole means of expression. It is not possible to identify cause and effect. So many developments were taking place at the same time that we can only point to the emergence, by the end of the nineteenth century, of a climate of largely unspoken opinion which had made English the natural choice for progress. We shall see this climate present in all of the domains reviewed in chapter 4.

'Unspoken' is an important word. Insofar as it is possible to find out about the decision-making processes which were taking place at the time, there is hardly any conscious justification for the role of English. When the first radio stations were coming on air, no one seems to have spent any time debating whether or not they should broadcast in English. There was plenty of discussion about what **kind** of English should be used, of course; but the choice of English in the first place was simply not an issue. Nor was it an issue for the other developments which were catching the public eye as the new century dawned.

There was nothing novel about taking English for granted in this way. Given the colonial origins of English in the countries of the inner circle, the standing of the language could never have been in doubt. There was no competition from other languages, no crisis of linguistic identity on the part of the colonial power, and thus no threat. No special mention is made of English in any of the documents which are significant for the history of Britain, and English has never been formally declared the official language of that country. Nor was English singled out for mention when the Constitution of the United States was being written. Rulings are needed to regulate conflict. If there is no conflict, there is no need for rulings.

However, as the twentieth century progressed, situations arose where repeatedly the status of English (and other ex-colonial languages) was called into question. The typical scenario was one where speakers of a language felt their language needed protection because its existence was being threatened by a more dominant language. In such cases, the dominant power would sometimes take measures to preserve it (usually, after forceful pressure from the members of the minority community) by giving it special recognition. This has happened occasionally, and especially in recent decades, among the countries of the inner circle: for example, some degree of official status has now been given to Welsh in Wales, Irish Gaelic in Ireland, French in Quebec, and Maori in New Zealand. And in each case, it has proved necessary to pay attention to the corresponding official role of English, in these territories, also as a protective measure. Here, the issue is one of identity.

Among the countries of the outer circle, where English is used as a second language, the decision to give English official status has usually been made in order to avoid the problem of having to choose between competing local languages. English is perceived to be a 'neutral' language, in this respect. Examples where this has happened include Ghana and Nigeria. Not everyone believes English to be neutral, of course, as we shall see in chapter 5, in relation to such cases as Kenya. But the decision, when it is made, is based on political expediency.

In a country where 95 per cent or so of the population speak English, as in Britain and the USA, it might be thought that a problem could not arise. But even small changes in the social balance of a population can have serious linguistic consequences. When large social changes take place, such as have happened through immigration during the past century, the potential effects on language policy and planning can be far-reaching, as we shall see later in relation to the current debate over the role of English in the USA.

But, in 1900, there was no prospect of any such debate. English had become the dominant language of global politics and economy, and all the signs were that it would remain so. Its status was not in question, and the role of the USA in its future was clear. A notable observation was that of Bismarck, who in 1898 was asked by a journalist what he considered to be the decisive factor in modern history; he replied, 'The fact that the North Americans speak English'. To maintain the standing of the language, all that was needed was a period of consolidation and expansion, and this, as the next chapter amply demonstrates, was soon forthcoming.

4

Why English?
The cultural legacy

The first steps in the political consolidation of English were taken during the decision-making which followed the First World War, in 1919. The mandates system introduced by the League of Nations transferred former German colonies in Africa, the Middle East, Asia, and the Pacific to the supervision of the victors, and English language influence grew immensely in the areas which came to be mediated directly by Britain (such as in Palestine, Cameroon and Tanganyika) or by other English-speaking nations: examples include Australia (in Papua New Guinea), New Zealand (in Western Samoa) and South Africa (in South-West Africa – present-day Namibia).

But the growth of linguistic influence through political expansion was already on the wane. Far more important for the English language, in the post-war world, was the way in which the cultural legacies of the colonial era and the technological revolution were being felt on an international scale. English was now emerging as a medium of communication in growth areas which would gradually shape the character of twentieth-century domestic and professional life.

International relations

The League of Nations was the first of many modern inter-national alliances to allocate a special place to English in its proceedings: English was one of the two official languages (the other was French), and all documents were printed in both. The League was created as part of the Treaty of Versailles in 1920, and at the time of its First Assembly, it had forty-two members, several from outside Europe. The importance of a lingua franca, with such an extended membership, was obvious. The League was replaced in 1945 by the United Nations, where the role of the lingua franca became even more critical. The UN now consists of over fifty distinct organs, programmes, and specialized agencies, as well as many regional and functional commissions, standing committees, expert bodies, and other organizations. English is one of the official languages within all of these structures.

The language plays an official or working role in the proceedings of most other major international political gatherings, in all parts of the world. Examples include the Association of South-East Asian Nations, the Commonwealth, the Council of Europe, the European Union and the North Atlantic Treaty Organization. English is the only official language of the Organization of Petroleum Exporting Countries, for example, and the only working language of the European Free Trade Association. Unless a body has a highly restricted membership (such as one consisting only of Arabic-speaking states or only of Spanish-speaking states), the choice of a lingua franca has to be made, and English is the first choice of most. However, even the restricted-membership meetings recognize the value of English: although their proceedings may not be expressed in English, the reports they issue for the wider public at the end of their meeting, and the statements which their officials make to the world media, usually are.

The extent to which English is used in this way is often not appreciated. In 1995–6, according to the Union of International Associations' *Yearbook*, there were about 12,500 international organizations in the world. About a third list the languages they use in an official or working capacity. A sample of 500 of these (taken from the beginning of the alphabet) showed that 85 per cent (424) made official use of English – far more than any other language. French was the only other language to show up strongly, with 49 per cent (245) using it officially. Thirty other languages also attracted occasional official status, but only Arabic, Spanish, and German achieved over 10 per cent recognition.

Of particular significance is the number of organizations in this sample which use **only** English to carry on their affairs: 169 – a third. This reliance is especially noticeable in Asia and the Pacific, where about 90 per cent of international bodies carry on their proceedings entirely in English. Many scientific organizations (such as the African Association of Science Editors, the Cairo Demographic Centre and Baltic Marine Biologists) are also English-only. By contrast, only a small number of international bodies (13 per cent) make no official use of English at all: most of these are French organizations, dealing chiefly with francophone concerns.

The reliance on English is by no means restricted to science, however. Several international sporting organizations work only in English, such as the African Hockey Federation, the Asian Amateur Athletic Association and the Association of Oceania National Olympic Committees; and when these organizations hold international competitions, the language automatically becomes the lingua franca of the gathering. English is used as the sole official language in relation to a wide range of topics, as is illustrated by the All-African People's Organization, Architects Regional Council Asia and the Asian Buddhist Conference for Peace.

These trends are reflected even in Europe, where we might expect other languages to be playing a more dominant role. We can see this if we examine the *Yearbook* organizations whose names begin with *Euro-*. Out of a sample of 1,000 of these, 440 specified the official or working languages they used. Almost all used English as an official language – 435, a remarkable 99 per cent. French was used by 63 per cent (278) and German by 40 per cent (176). English + French + German was the most popular European combination.

In Europe, too, organizations which work only in English are surprisingly common, especially in science. The European Academy of Anaesthesiology and the European Academy of Facial Surgery use only English in their proceedings, as do the

European Association of Cancer Research and the European Association of Fish Pathology. Bodies from other domains include the European Air Law Association, the European Bridge League and the European Aluminium Association. One of the few organizations which makes no official use of English at all is the European Federation of Perfumery Retailers.

Several bodies use English in more than one way. For example, the Afro-Asian Rural Reconstruction Organization has three official languages – English, Arabic and French – but for its working language it uses only English. Europage, which unites the yellow-pages publishers of the European Union, lists Dutch, English, French, German, Italian and Spanish as official languages, but adds that only English is to be used for correspondence.

The overriding impression is that, wherever in the world an organization is based, English is the chief auxiliary language. The Andean Commission of Jurists recognizes Spanish – and English. The German anatomical association Anatomische Gesellschaft recognizes German – and English. The Arab Air Carriers Association recognizes Arabic – and English.

A different kind of role for English is encountered at meetings where a large number of nations each has the right to participate using its own language. The European Union is the most complex example, where eleven member states (in 1995) were presenting a situation in which as many as 110 pairs of languages require translation services (French/English, French/German, French/Finnish, etc.). It is impossible to find expert translators for all language pairs, or to provide maximum coverage on all occasions, so efforts have been made to find alternative procedures (other than asking some of the countries to give up their official status).

One solution is the use of a 'relay' system. If there is no Finnish/Greek translator available, for instance, English might be used as an intermediary language – or 'interlingua', as it is sometimes called. One person would translate a speech from Finnish into English; another would translate the result from English into Greek. Any language could be so used, but English is the one which seems to be most often employed in this way. In 1995, according to the European Bureau of Lesser Used Languages, 42 per cent of European Union citizens claimed to be able to converse in English – well ahead of German (31 per cent) and French (29 per cent).

International politics operates at several levels and in many different ways, but the presence of English is usually not far away. A political protest may surface in the form of an official question to a government minister, a peaceful lobby outside an embassy, a street riot, or a bomb. When the television cameras present the event to a world audience, it is notable how often a message in English can be seen on a banner or placard as part of the occasion. Whatever the mother tongue of the protesters, they know that their cause will gain maximum impact if it is expressed through the medium of English. A famous instance of this occurred a few years ago in India, where a march supporting Hindi and opposing English was seen on world television: most of the banners were in Hindi, but one astute marcher carried a prominent sign which read 'Death to English' – thereby enabling the voice of his group to reach much further around the world than would otherwise have been possible.

The media

These days, any consideration of politics leads inevitably to a consideration of the role of the media. Indeed, if the erstwhile anonymous author of the novel *Primary Colours* (1996) is to be believed, successful access to the media is the guarantor of political achievement, and much of a campaign staff member's time is devoted to ensuring that this will happen. At one point (p. 330), Henry Burton, the governor's aide, reflects ruefully on the way the election campaign was going wrong:

The Sunday morning papers had Freddie Picker being endorsed by the governor of Pennsylvania and most of the state's congressional delegation. I read it as a civilian might, without a twinge. There had been days, *months*, when I could soar or dive on the hint of a nuance in a one-paragraph item buried in *The Washington Post*; that had been my life. But the campaign was over for me now.

82

In the novel, the media are at the centre of everyone's life – the press, radio, advertising, and especially television. Even the 'hint of a nuance' can make a difference.

- *The press*

The English language has been an important medium of the press for nearly 400 years. As early as the first decades of the seventeenth century, several European countries were publishing rudimentary newspapers, but censorship, taxation, wars, and other constraints allowed little growth. Progress was much greater in Britain, though even in that country periods of censorship greatly limited newspaper content until towards the end of the century. The *Weekley Newes* began to appear (irregularly) from 1622; the *London Gazette* in 1666; and *Lloyd's News* in 1696, providing general news as well as information about shipping. American developments, beginning somewhat later, included the *Boston News-Letter* (1704), *The New-York Gazette* (1725), and the New York City *Daily Advertiser* (1785). The beginning of the eighteenth century in Britain saw the rise and fall of *The Tatler* (1709) and *The Spectator* (1711), while the end brought the arrival of *The Times* (1788) and *The Observer* (1791).

The nineteenth century was the period of greatest progress, thanks to the introduction of new printing technology and new methods of mass production and transportation. It also saw the development of a truly independent press, chiefly fostered in the USA, where there were some 400 daily newspapers by 1850, and nearly 2,000 by the turn of the century. Censorship and other restrictions continued in Continental Europe during the early decades, however, which meant that the provision of popular news in languages other than English developed much more slowly.

Massive circulations were achieved by such papers as the *New York Herald* (1833) and *New York Tribune* (1841). Sensationalism brought even larger sales, and newspaper empires grew. In Britain, taxation restricted the growth of the press in the first half of the century, but *The Times* continued to grow in stature throughout the period, and the abolition of the Stamp Tax in

1855 prompted a flood of publications. By the end of the century, popular journalism, in the form of *The Daily Mail* (1896), brought Britain into line with America. From then on, no headlines screamed with greater visual force from the news-stands of the world than those published in the English language.

The high profile given to English in the popular press was reinforced by the way techniques of news gathering developed. The mid nineteenth century saw the growth of the major news agencies, especially following the invention of the telegraph (they were long known as 'wire services'). Paul Julius Reuter started an office in Aachen, but soon moved to London, where in 1851 he launched the agency which now bears his name. By 1870 Reuters had acquired more territorial news monopolies than any of its Continental competitors. With the emergence in 1856 of the New York Associated Press (which later developed into the Associated Press), the majority of the information being transmitted along the telegraph wires of the world was in English.

Newspapers are not solely international media: they play an important role in the identity of a local community. Most papers are for home circulation, and are published in a home language. It is therefore impossible to gain an impression of the power of English from the bare statistics of newspaper production and circulation. None the less, according to the data compiled by the *Encyclopedia Britannica*, in 1994 about a third of the world's newspapers were being published in those countries (see the list at the end of chapter 2) where the English language has special status, and it is reasonable to assume that the majority of these would be in English.

More important – though much more subjective – are estimates of the influence of individual newspapers on a world scale. In one such table, reported in the *Book of Lists* (1977), the top five papers were all in English: top was *The New York Times*, followed by *The Washington Post*, *The Wall Street Journal*, and the two British papers *The Times* and *The Sunday Times*. Of particular importance are those English-language newspapers intended for a global readership, such as the *International Herald-Tribune*, *US Weekly* and *International Guardian*.

A similar story could be told in relation to the publication of periodicals, magazines, pamphlets, digests and other ephemera. Information is much more sparse (only half the countries in the world have provided data for comparative listings), but it would seem that about a quarter of the world's periodicals are published in English-status countries. This total refers to all kinds of publication, of course – literary reviews, hobby journals, comics, fanzines (fan group magazines), pornographic literature, technical reviews, scholarly journals and much more.

When the focus is restricted to individual genres, the figures vary dramatically. As a visit to any university library shows, in any country, most academic journals with an international readership are published in English. The journal *Linguistics Abstracts* reviews the content of some 160 linguistics journals worldwide: nearly 70 per cent are published entirely in English. In the physical sciences, the figure may reach 80 per cent or more. By contrast, material aimed at younger people, such as comics and fanzines, is often in a local language.

- *Advertising*

Towards the end of the nineteenth century, a combination of social and economic factors led to a dramatic increase in the use of advertisements in publications, especially in the more industrialized countries. Mass production had increased the flow of goods and was fostering competition; consumer purchasing power was growing; and new printing techniques were providing fresh display possibilities. In the USA, publishers realized that income from advertising would allow them to lower the selling price of their magazine, and thus hugely increase circulation. In 1893 *McClure's Magazine*, *Cosmopolitan* and *Munsey's Magazine* all adopted this tactic, and within a few years, the 'ten-cent magazine' had trebled its sales. Before long, publications in which over half of the pages were given over to advertising became the norm, from the turn of the century increasingly in colour, leading eventually to the arrival of the wide range of glossy magazines and newspaper supplements available today. Two-thirds of a modern newspaper, especially in the USA, may be devoted to advertising.

English in advertising began very early on, when the weekly

newspapers began to carry items about books, medicines, tea, and other domestic products. An advertising supplement appeared in the *London Gazette* in 1666, and within a century advertisements had grown both in number and in style – so much so that Dr Johnson was led to comment caustically about their 'magnificence of promise and . . . eloquence sometimes sublime and sometimes pathetic'. During the nineteenth century the advertising slogan became a feature of the medium, as did the famous 'trade name'. 'It pays to advertise' itself became a US slogan in the 1920s. Many products which are now household names received a special boost in that decade, such as Ford, Coca Cola, Kodak and Kellogg.

The media capitalized on the brevity with which a product could be conveyed to an audience – even if the people were passing at speed in one of the new methods of transportation. Posters, billboards, electric displays, shop signs and other techniques became part of the everyday scene. As international markets grew, the 'outdoor media' began to travel the world, and their prominence in virtually every town and city is now one of the most noticeable global manifestations of English language use. The English advertisements are not always more numerous, in countries where English has no special status, but they are usually the most noticeable.

In all of this, it is the English of American products which rules. During the 1950s, the proportion of gross national income devoted to advertising was much higher in the USA than anywhere else: in 1953, for example, it was 2.6 per cent, compared with 1.5 per cent in Britain. Nearly $6,000 million were devoted to advertising in the USA in 1950, and this rapidly increased as advertisers began to see the potential of television. Other languages began to feel the effects: in Italian, a single verb sums up the era: *cocacolonizzare*, based on *coca cola* and *colonize*.

The impact was less marked in Europe, where TV advertising was more strictly controlled, but once commercial channels developed, there was a rapid period of catching up, in which American experience and influence were pervasive. The advertising agencies came into their own. By 1972, only three of the world's top thirty agencies were not US-owned (two in Japan and one in Britain). The official language of international advertising bodies, such as the European Association of Advertising Agencies, is invariably English.

- *Broadcasting*

It took many decades of experimental research in physics, chiefly in Britain and America, before it was possible to send the first radio telecommunication signals through the air, without wires (hence the name 'wireless telegraphy'). Marconi's system, built in 1895, carried telegraph code signals over a distance of one mile. Six years later, his signals had crossed the Atlantic Ocean; by 1918, they had reached Australia. English was the first language to be transmitted by radio, when US physicist Reginald A. Fessenden broadcast music, poetry, and a short talk to Atlantic shipping from Brant Rock, Massachusetts, USA, on Christmas Eve 1906.

Within twenty-five years of Marconi's first transmission, public broadcasting became a reality. The first commercial radio station was KDKA in Pittsburgh, Pennsylvania, which broadcast its first programme in November 1920 – an account of the Harding–Cox presidential election results. By 1922, in the USA, over 500 broadcasting stations had been licensed; and by 1995, the total was around 5,000 (each for AM and for FM commercial stations). Advertising revenue eventually became the chief means of support, as it later did for television.

In Britain, experimental broadcasts were being made as early as 1919, and the British Broadcasting Company (later, Corporation) was established in 1922. It was a monopoly: no other broadcasting company was allowed until the creation of the Independent Television Authority in 1954. In contrast with the USA, BBC revenue came not from advertising, but from royalties on broadcasting equipment and a public licence system (eventually the only revenue). The first director-general of the BBC, John Reith, developed a concept of public-service broadcasting – to inform, educate, and entertain – which proved to be highly influential abroad.

During the early 1920s, English-language broadcasting began

in Canada, Australia and New Zealand. The Indian Broadcasting Company had stations in Bombay and Calcutta by 1927. Most European countries commenced radio services during the same period. As services proliferated, the need for international agreements (for example, over the use of wavelengths) became urgent. Several organizations now exist, the largest being the International Telecommunications Union, created as early as 1865 to handle the problems of telegraphy.

There are also several important regional organizations, such as the Commonwealth Broadcasting Association and the European Broadcasting Union, as well as cultural and educational organizations, such as the London-based International Broadcast Institute. In these cases, we find a growing reliance on English as a lingua franca, corresponding to that found in the world of international politics. The Asia–Pacific Broadcasting Union, for example, uses only English as an official language.

A similar dramatic expansion later affected public television. The world's first high-definition service, provided by the BBC, began in London in 1936. In the USA, the National Broadcasting Company was able to provide a regular service in 1939. Within a year there were over twenty TV stations operating in the USA, and although the constraints imposed by the Second World War brought a setback, by 1995 the total number of stations had grown to over 1500. Ten million TV receivers were in use by 1951; by 1990 the figure was approaching 200 million. There was a proportional growth in Britain, which had issued over 300,000 TV licences by 1950. Other countries were much slower to enter the television age, and none has ever achieved the levels of outreach found in the USA, where on average in 1994 there was almost one receiver per person, and, again on average, each person spent almost 1,000 hours watching TV during the year.

We can only speculate about how these media developments must have influenced the growth of world English. A casual pass through the wavelengths of a radio receiver shows that no one language rules the airwaves, and there are no statistics on the proportion of time devoted to English-language programmes the world over, or on how much time is spent listening to such programmes. Only a few indirect indications exist: for example, in

1994 about 45 per cent of the world's radio receivers were in those countries where the English language has a special status; but what such figures say in real terms about exposure to English is anyone's guess.

A more specific indication is broadcasting aimed specifically at audiences in other countries. Such programmes were introduced in the 1920s, but Britain did not develop its services until the next decade. The international standing of BBC programmes, especially its news broadcasts, achieved a high point during the Second World War, when they helped to raise morale in German-occupied territories. The World Service of the BBC, launched (as the Empire Service) in 1932, though much cut back in recent years, in early 1996 was still broadcasting over 1,000 hours per week to a worldwide audience of 140 million in over forty countries – nearly a third in English. BBC English Radio produces over 100 hours of bilingual and all-English programmes weekly. London Radio Services, a publicly funded radio syndicator, offers a daily international news service to over 10,000 radio stations worldwide, chiefly in English

Although later to develop, the USA rapidly overtook Britain, becoming the leading provider of English-language services abroad. The Voice of America, the external broadcasting service of the US Information Agency, was not founded until 1942, but it came into its own during the Cold War years. By the 1980s, it was broadcasting from the USA worldwide in English and forty-five other languages. Along with the foreign-based Radio Liberty and Radio Free Europe, the US output amounted to nearly 2,000 hours a week – not far short of the Soviet Union's total. Other sources include the American Forces Radio and Television Service, which broadcasts through a network of local stations all over the world. The International Broadcast Station offers a shortwave service to Latin America in English and certain other languages. Radio New York World Wide provides an English-language service to Europe, Africa and the Caribbean. And channels with a religious orientation also often broadcast widely in English: for example, World International Broadcasters transmits to Europe, the Middle East, and North Africa.

Most other countries showed sharp increases in external

broadcasting during the post-War years, and several launched English-language radio programmes, such as the Soviet Union, Italy, Japan, Luxembourg, The Netherlands, Germany and Sweden. No comparative data are available about how many people listen to each of the languages provided by these services. However, if we list the languages in which these countries broadcast, it is noticeable that only one of these languages has a place on each of the lists: English.

• *Motion pictures*

The new technologies which followed the discovery of electrical power fundamentally altered the nature of home and public entertainment, and provided fresh directions for the development of the English language. Broadcasting was obviously one of these, but that medium was never – according to the influential views of Lord Reith – to be identified solely with the provision of entertainment. This observation did not apply in the case of the motion picture industry.

The technology of this industry has many roots in Europe and America during the nineteenth century, with England and France providing an initial impetus to the artistic and commercial development of the cinema from 1895. However, the years preceding and during the First World War stunted the growth of a European film industry, and dominance soon passed to America, which oversaw from 1915 the emergence of the feature film, the star system, the movie mogul, and the grand studio, all based in Hollywood, California.

As a result, when sound was added to the technology in the late 1920s, it was the English language which suddenly came to dominate the movie world. It is difficult to find accurate data, but several publications of the period provide clues. For example, in 1933 appeared the first edition of *The Picturegoer's Who's Who and Encyclopaedia of the Screen Today*. Of the 44 studios listed, 32 were American or British (the others were German and French). Of the 2,466 artistes listed, only 85 (3 per cent) were making movies in languages other than English. Of the 340 directors, 318 (94 per cent) were involved only in English-language works.

As an English-language reference book, there is bound to be some bias in the coverage - few movie stars are listed from non-European countries, for example – but the overall impression is probably not far from the truth.

Despite the growth of the film industry in other countries in later decades, English-language movies still dominate the medium, with Hollywood coming to rely increasingly on a small number of annual productions aimed at huge audiences – such as *Jurassic Park*, *Aladdin* and *Forrest Gump*. It is unusual to find a blockbuster movie produced in a language other than English. In 1994, according to the listings in the *BFI Film and Television Handbook* for 1996, 80 per cent of all feature films given a theatrical release were in English. The Oscar system has always been English-language oriented (though the category of best foreign film was recognized in 1947), but there is a strong English-language presence in most other film festivals too. Half of the Best Film awards ever given at the Cannes Film Festival, for example, have been to English-language productions.

By the mid-1990s, according to film critic David Robinson in an *Encyclopedia Britannica* (1995) review, the USA controlled about 85 per cent of the world film market, with Hollywood films dominating the box offices in most countries. A cinema in Denmark would very likely be showing the same range of films as one in Spain, and most would be English-language films (usually subtitled). A notable development was to see this dominance manifest itself even in countries where there has been a strong national tradition of film-making, such as Japan, France, Italy and Germany. Before 1990, France was continuing to attract majority audiences for its own films (the only European country to do so); in recent years, French-language films may account for as little as 30 per cent of the national box office.

The influence of movies on the viewing audience is uncertain, but many observers agree with the view of the German director Wim Wenders: 'People increasingly believe in what they see and they buy what they believe in . . . People use, drive, wear, eat and buy what they see in the movies.' If this is so, then the fact that most movies are made in the English language must surely be significant, at least in the long term.

- *Popular music*

The cinema was one of two new entertainment technologies which emerged at the end of the nineteenth century: the other was the recording industry. Here too the English language was early in evidence. When in 1877 Thomas A. Edison devised the phonograph, the first machine that could both record and reproduce sound, the first words to be recorded were 'What God hath wrought', followed by the words of the nursery-rhyme 'Mary had a little lamb'.

Most of the subsequent technical developments took place in the USA. Gramophone records soon came to replace cylinders. The first US patent for magnetic tape was as early as 1927. Columbia Records introduced the long-playing (LP) disk in 1948. All the major recording companies in popular music had English-language origins. The oldest active record label is the US firm Columbia (from 1898); others are HMV (originally British), merged in 1931 with Columbia to form EMI. Other labels include Brunswick, established in the USA in 1916, and Decca, established in Britain in 1929.

Radio sets around the world hourly testify to the dominance of English in the popular music scene today. Many people make their first contact with English in this way. It is a dominance which is a specifically twentieth-century phenomenon, but the role of English in this genre starts much earlier. During the nineteenth century, popular music was embedded within the dance halls, beer halls, and popular theatres of innumerable European cities, producing thousands of songs whose content ranged from the wildly comic and satirical to the desperately sentimental. The British music hall was a major influence on popular trends – much more so, it is thought, than the French and German cabarets and operettas of the period.

Travelling British entertainers visited the USA, which developed its own music hall traditions in the form of vaudeville. Touring minstrel groups became popular from the middle of the century. Songwriters such as Stephen Foster found their compositions (over 200 hits, including 'Old Folks at Home', 'Camptown Races', and 'Beautiful Dreamer') circulating on an unprecedented scale through the rapidly growing network of theatres. By the turn of the century, Tin Pan Alley (the popular name for the Broadway-centered song-publishing industry) was a reality, and was soon known worldwide as the chief source of US popular music.

A similar trend can be seen in relation to the more 'up-market' genres. During the early twentieth century, European light opera (typified by Strauss and Offenbach) developed an English-language dimension. Several major composers were immigrants to the USA, such as the Czech-born Rudolf Friml (who arrived in 1906) and Hungarian-born Sigmund Romberg (who arrived in 1909), or they were the children of immigrants (such as George Gershwin). The 1920s proved to be a remarkable decade for the operetta, as a result, with such famous examples as Romberg's *The Student Prince* (1924) and Friml's *Rose Marie*. The same decade also saw the rapid growth of the musical, a distinctively US product, and the rise to fame of such composers as Jerome Kern and George Gershwin, and later Cole Porter and Richard Rodgers.

The rapidly growing broadcasting companies were greedy for fresh material, and thousands of new works each year found an international audience in ways that could not have been conceived of a decade before. The availability of mass-produced gramophone records allowed the works of these composers ('songs from the shows') to travel the world in physical form. Soon the words of the hit songs were being learned by heart and reproduced with varying accents in cabarets and music halls all over Europe – as well as in the homes of the well-to-do.

Jazz, too, influenced so much by the folk blues of black plantation workers, had its linguistic dimension. Blues singers such as Ma Rainey and Bessie Smith were part of the US music-hall scene from the early years of the twentieth century. Other genres emerged – hillbilly songs, country music, gospel songs, and a wide range of folk singing. The vocal element in the dance music of such swing bands as Glenn Miller's swept the world in the 1930s and 1940s. And, in due course, the words and beat of rhythm and blues grew into rock and roll.

When modern popular music arrived, it was almost entirely an

English scene. The pop groups of two chief English-speaking nations were soon to dominate the recording world: Bill Haley and the Comets and Elvis Presley in the USA; the Beatles and the Rolling Stones in the UK. Mass audiences for pop singers became a routine feature of the world scene from the 1960s. No other single source has spread the English language around the youth of the world so rapidly and so pervasively. In 1996, Nick Reynolds, a popular music producer of the BBC World Service, writing in the English-speaking Union's periodical *Concord*, commented: 'Pop music is virtually the only field in which the British have led the world in the past three decades', and adds, echoing the accolade made some 200 years ago (p. 71), 'Britain is still the pop workshop of the planet'.

In the 1990s, the English-language character of the international pop music world is extraordinary. Although every country has its popular singers, singing in their own language, only a few manage to break through into the international arena, and in order to do so it seems they need to be singing in English. The 1990 edition of *The Penguin Encyclopedia of Popular Music* is an instructive guide: of the 557 pop groups it includes, 549 (99 per cent) work entirely or predominantly in English; of the 1,219 solo vocalists, 1,156 (95 per cent) sing in English. The mother tongue of the singers is apparently irrelevant. The entire international career of ABBA, the Swedish group with over twenty hit records in the 1970s, was in English.

These days, the sound of the English language, through the medium of popular song, is heard wherever there is a radio set. It is a commonplace tourist experience to hear a familiar English refrain in a coffee bar, bus station or elevator, or simply issuing from the window of a house on almost any street in any town. Often, it is a source of despair. We travel to 'get away from it all', and 'it' follows us everywhere we go. We enter a local night-club in our holiday destination, and all we hear is the current top twenty. 'Happy birthday to you' is widely sung at children's birthday parties. Finding genuinely local music can be extremely difficult. Several commentators have remarked on the way in which western popular music has threatened the life of ethnic musical traditions everywhere.

At the same time, other commentators have drawn attention to the way popular music in the English language has had a profound and positive impact on the nature of modern popular culture in general. As the lyrics (as distinct from the tunes) of Bob Dylan, Bob Marley, John Lennon, Joan Baez and others spread around the world, during the 1960s and 1970s, English for the younger generation in many countries became a symbol of freedom, rebellion and modernism. The social, political, and spiritual messages carried by the words (such as 'We Shall Overcome') resounded at gatherings in many countries, providing many people with a first – and often highly charged – experience of the unifying power of English in action. And the language has continued to play this role, being the medium of such international projects as 'Live Aid'.

International travel

The reasons for travelling abroad are many and various. They range from routine business trips to annual holidays, and from religious pilgrimages and sports competitions to military interventions. Each journey has immediate linguistic consequences – a language has to be interpreted, learned, imposed – and over time a travelling trend can develop into a major influence. If there is a contemporary movement towards world English use, therefore, we would expect it to be particularly noticeable in this domain. And so it is.

In the tourist industry, for example, worldwide international arrivals passed 500 million in 1993. The leading tourism earner and spender is the USA. In 1992, according to the World Tourism Organization, the USA earned over 50,000 million dollars from tourism – twice as much as its nearest rival, France; it also spent nearly 40,000 million on tourism – ahead of Germany and Japan. Money talks very loudly in tourism – if only because the tourist has extra money to spend while on holiday. In the tourist spots of the world, accordingly, the signs in the shop windows are most commonly in English. Restaurant menus tend to have a parallel version in English. Credit card facilities, such as American Express and Mastercard, are most noticeably in

English. And among the destitute who haunt the tourist locations, the smattering of foreign language which is used to sell artefacts or to beg money from the passing visitor is usually a pidgin form of English.

Move away from the regular tourist routes, however, and English soon becomes conspicuous by its absence. It is important not to forget the fact that, even if one third of the world is now regularly exposed to English, as was suggested in chapter 1, this still means that two thirds are not. We need only to walk up a side street in a city, or pause at a village on our way to a destination, to experience the world's remarkable linguistic diversity. The more we know about the language(s) of the country we are exploring, the more we shall be rewarded with a visit that is insightful and comfortable.

By contrast, for those whose international travel brings them into a world of package holidays, business meetings, academic conferences, international conventions, community rallies, sporting occasions, military occupations and other 'official' gatherings, the domains of transportation and accommodation are mediated through the use of English as an auxiliary language. Safety instructions on international flights and sailings, information about emergency procedures in hotels, and directions to major locations are now increasingly in English alongside local languages. Most notices which tell us to fasten our seatbelts, find the lifeboat stations, or check the location of the emergency stairs give us an option in English. In some cities, the trend towards English has been especially noticeable. An English-speaking visitor to Tokyo in 1985 would have found city travel a largely impenetrable experience without an English-language map; but by 1995, English road signs had become commonplace.

The role of the military, in the spread of English, is difficult to evaluate. It is obvious that the language of an invading army, or an army of occupation, must have an immediate effect on a community, but how long this effect lasts is an open question. American songs were exported both in the Boer War and the First World War, and American Forces Network radio, in particular, ensured that English was widely heard in Europe during and after World War II. The presence of US and British forces in large numbers would certainly have brought the local inhabitants into contact with English-speaking culture more rapidly than would otherwise have been the case, if only in such areas as advertising and popular music. It is even possible that in some instances the effects would be long-lasting – perhaps as individuals returned to marry or work in a former war zone. This especially happened in Europe after 1945. But there is little evidence to go on.

A similar point could be made about the 1990s, which has seen the presence of English-speaking troops on peace-keeping missions in Bosnia, the Middle East, Central Africa and elsewhere. UN officers are routinely heard on TV commenting on the way a crisis is developing, and the language used to the cameras is almost always English. But is it likely that an English-language presence of a few months, or even years, would have a long-term influence on local language awareness? We can only speculate.

International safety

A special aspect of safety is the way that the language has come to be used as a means of controlling international transport operations, especially on water and in the air. As world travel has grown, more people and goods are being transported more quickly and simultaneously to more places than ever before. The communicative demands placed on air and sea personnel, given the variety of language backgrounds involved, have thus grown correspondingly. In such circumstances, the use of a lingua franca has proved of great worth.

English has long been recognized as the international language of the sea, and in recent years there have been attempts to refine its use to make it as efficient as possible. Larger and faster ships pose greater navigational hazards. Shipping routes continually alter and present fresh problems of traffic flow. Radio and satellite systems have greatly extended a ship's communicative range. In such circumstances, mariners need to make their speech clear and unambiguous, to reduce the possibility of confusion in the sending and receiving of messages.

In 1980, a project was set up to produce Essential English for

International Maritime Use – often referred to as 'Seaspeak'. The recommendations related mainly to communication by VHF radio, and included procedures for initiating, maintaining, and terminating conversations, as well as a recommended grammar, vocabulary and structure for messages on a wide range of maritime subjects. For example, instead of saying 'What did you say?', 'I didn't hear you', 'Would you please say that once more', and many other possibilities, Seaspeak recommends a single phrase: 'Say again'. Likewise, bearings and courses are given with three-figure values ('009 degrees', not '9 degrees') and dates are signalled using prefixes ('day one-three, month zero-five, year one-nine-nine-six'). Though it is far more restricted than every-day language, Seaspeak has considerable expressive power.

Progress has also been made in recent years in devising systems of unambiguous communication between organizations which are involved in handling emergencies on the ground – notably, the fire serice, the ambulance service and the police. When the Channel Tunnel between England and France came into operation for the first time in 1994, it presented new possibilities for international confusion. Research has therefore been ongoing into a way of standardizing communication between the UK and the Continent of Europe: it is called 'Emergencyspeak'.

A great deal of the motivation for these restricted languages – and a major influence on their phraseology – has come from the language of air traffic control, which presents international safety with its greatest challenge. Far more nations are forced to make routine daily communications with each other in relation to air transportation than ever occurs on the sea. Only a handful of nations are truly seafaring; but all nations are nowadays airborne. And the pace of change here has been truly phenomenal. In 1940, US air carriers were handling around 2 million passengers a year in about 350 planes; in 1950 the totals had grown to some 17 million in over 1,000 planes. In 1994 the number of passengers worldwide exceeded 1,200 million.

The official use of English as the language of international aircraft control did not emerge until after the Second World War. Allied leaders organized a conference in Chicago in 1944 at which they laid the foundations for the post-war global civil aviation system, creating the International Civil Aviation Organization. Seven years later they agreed that English should be the international language of aviation when pilots and controllers speak different languages. This would have been the obvious choice for a lingua franca. The leaders of the Allies were English-speaking; the major aircraft manufacturers were English-speaking; and most of the post-war pilots in the West (largely ex-military personnel) were English-speaking.

The arguments in favour of a single language of air traffic control are obvious. It is safer if all pilots understand all conversations. Pilots who have a two-way radio are required to keep a listening watch at all times on the appropriate frequency. They listen not only to messages addressed to themselves, but also to messages being sent to and from other pilots in their neighbourhood. In this way they can learn about weather and traffic conditions from other pilots, without having to keep referring to air traffic control. Furthermore, if they hear an error in someone else's conversation, they can draw attention to it. If more than one language is being used, the risk of a breakdown in communication inevitably increases.

There have however been several cases where the case for bilingual air traffic control has been strongly argued, and sometimes this has led to a difficult political situation (such as the strike by pilots and air traffic controllers over a bilingual policy in Quebec, Canada, in 1976). Supporters of bilingual air traffic control stress the fact that not all pilots have a good command of English. They may have a poor pronunciation, which is made even more difficult for a controller to understand by the presence of background aircraft noise and the effects of stress on the voice. Pilots also may have difficulty understanding a controller, for the same reasons. Under such circumstances, it has been argued, it may actually be safer if both parties are allowed to communicate fluently with each other in a language they both understand well.

These arguments are still encountered in parts of the world where bilingual identity is critical, and two languages are officially used in certain localities (such as the use of French at Montreal). But in general the strength of the argument for a single language of air traffic control is not questioned, nor is the role of English. However, the issue is not simply to do with choosing one language; it is far more to do with moulding that language so that it is suitable for its purpose – economical and precise communication, to ensure safety at all times.

Even within a single language, terminology and phrasing need to be standardized, to avoid ambiguity, and great efforts have been made to develop such a system for English, widely called 'Airspeak'. Everyone knows – if only from the movies – that pilots do not talk in a normal way to air traffic control. They use a restricted vocabulary and a fixed set of sentence patterns which aim to express unambiguously all possible air situations. They include terms such as 'Roger', 'Wilco', and 'Mayday'; phrases such as 'Maintaining 2500 feet' and 'Runway in sight'; and the use of a phonetic alphabet to spell out codenames ('Alpha, Bravo, Charlie, Delta . . . ').

Over 180 nations have adopted the recommendations of the International Civil Aviation Organization (ICAO) about English terminology. However, there is nothing mandatory about them (nor about Seaspeak, and other such systems). Even the US Federal Aviation Administration uses wording which differs from ICAO's in many instances. A proposal for a new international glossary is currently being discussed. The problem is plain: it is relatively easy to set up a working party which will compile a single terminology for world use; the difficulty comes in persuading everyone to comply with it (which is likely to mean changing a country's traditional practice).

Under these circumstances, rather than try to impose a single Airspeak on everyone, some authorities think that it may be more satisfactory, in the long term, to work towards improving the quality of English used by air personnel. There are currently no agreed international standards for aviation English, or tests that all pilots have to take. And although most pilots' level of English is far greater than the level required by Airspeak norms, many would find it difficult to use English in any daily circumstance outside of that used in aircraft communication.

Arguments about safety involve many factors, and it is difficult to isolate one (such as language) and rely on it entirely. But there are some famous cases where the primary cause of the accident does seem to have been linguistic. In 1977, unclear English accents and terminology caused the collision between two Boeing 747s on the foggy runway at Tenerife – the worst disaster in aviation history. A KLM captain thought the Spanish controller had cleared him for take-off, whereas the controller had intended only to give departure instructions. In 1995, poor communication caused an American Airlines plane to crash at Cali, Colombia. An accident prevention study carried out by Boeing found that, in the decade 1982–1991, pilot–controller miscommunication contributed to at least 11 per cent of fatal crashes worldwide.

People have used cases of this kind to argue in support of bilingual air traffic control, or the use of a simpler auxiliary language such as Esperanto. But it seems likely that the problem of poor accents, background noise, and other variables would present difficulties, regardless of the language in use. In the meantime, English – with all its failings – remains the recommended language of international air travel.

Education

It follows from what has been said in this chapter that English is the medium of a great deal of the world's knowledge, especially in such areas as science and technology. And access to knowledge is the business of education. When we investigate why so many nations have in recent years made English an official language or chosen it as their chief foreign language in schools, one of the most important reasons is always educational – in the broadest sense. Black South African writer Harry Mashabela, writing in 1975, puts it like this:

learning and using English will not only give us the much-needed unifying chord but will also land us into the exciting world of ideas; it will enable us to keep company with kings in the world of ideas and also make it possible for us to share the experiences of our own brothers in the world . . .

And Sridath Ramphal, writing in 1996, adds an anecdote:

shortly after I became Secretary-General of the Commonwealth in 1975, I met Prime Minister Sirimavo Bandaranaike in Colombo and we talked of ways in which the Commonwealth Secretariat could help Sri Lanka. Her response was immediate and specific: 'Send us people to train our teachers to teach English as a foreign language'. My amazement must have showed, for the Prime Minister went on to explain that the policies her husband had put in place twenty years earlier to promote Sinhalese as the official language had succeeded so well that in the process Sri Lanka – so long the pearl of the English-speaking world in Asia – had in fact lost English, even as a second language save for the most educated Sri Lankans. Her concern was for development. Farmers in the field, she told me, could not read the instructions on bags of imported fertiliser – and manufacturers in the global market were not likely to print them in Sinhalese. Sri Lanka was losing its access to the world language of English. We did respond. I believe that today English is doing better as the second language in Sri Lanka.

Not everyone has viewed the arrival of the language in such a positive light, as we shall see in chapter 5; but the dominant view is certainly that a person is more likely to be in touch with the latest thinking and research in a subject by learning English than by learning any other language.

It is important to appreciate that the use of English does vary, in this respect. A 1981 study of the use of English in scientific periodicals showed that 85 per cent of papers in biology and physics were being written in English at that time, whereas medical papers were some way behind (73 per cent), and papers in mathematics and chemistry further behind still (69 per cent and 67 per cent respectively). However, all these areas had shown a significant increase in their use of English during the preceding fifteen years – over 30 per cent, in the case of chemistry, and over 40 per cent, in the case of medicine – and the figures fifteen years further on would certainly be much higher. This can be seen even in a language-sensitive subject such as linguistics, where in 1995 nearly 90 per cent of the 1,500 papers listed in the journal *Linguistics Abstracts* were in English. In computer science, the proportion is even higher.

Since the 1960s, English has become the normal medium of instruction in higher education for many countries – including several where the language has no official status. Advanced courses in The Netherlands, for example, are widely taught in English. If most students are going to encounter English routinely in their monographs and periodicals, it is suggested – an argument which is particularly cogent in relation to the sciences – then it makes sense to teach advanced courses in that language, to better prepare them for that encounter. But these days there is also a strong lingua franca argument: the pressure to use English has grown as universities and colleges have increasingly welcomed foreign students, and lecturers have found themselves faced with mixed-language audiences.

The English language teaching (ELT) business has become one of the major growth industries around the world in the past thirty years. An illustration of the scale of the development can be seen from the work of The British Council, which in 1996 had a network of offices in 109 countries promoting cultural, educational and technical cooperation, In 1995–6, over 400,000 candidates worldwide sat English language examinations administered by the Council, over half of these being examinations in English as a foreign language. At any one time during that year, there were 120,000 students learning English and other skills through the medium of English in Council teaching centres. With thousands of other schools and centres worldwide now also devoted to English-language teaching, the Council has estimated that, by the year 2000, there will be over 1,000 million people learning English.

In a 1995 global consultation exercise initiated by *English 2000*, a British Council project, people professionally involved in ELT in some ninety countries were asked to react to a series of statements concerning the role and future of the English language. Responses used a 5-point scale from 'strongly agree' to 'strongly disagree'. Nearly 1,400 questionnaires were returned. One of the statements was: 'The global market for English language teaching and learning will increase over the next 25 years.' Over 93 per cent agreed or strongly agreed. A particular growth area is central and eastern Europe, and the countries of the former Soviet Union, where it is thought that nearly 10 per cent of the population – some 50 million in all – are now learning English.

Certain other statements in the Council questionnaire were also given an unequivocal response. They included:

- English will retain its role as the dominant language in world media and communications. 94 per cent agreed or strongly agreed.
- English is essential for progress as it will provide the main means of access to high-tech communication and information over the next twenty-five years. 95 per cent agreed or strongly agreed.
- English will remain the world's language for international communication for the next twenty-five years. 96 per cent agreed or strongly agreed.

Exercises of this kind have no clear predictive value, but they do provide a useful glimpse of the way specialists are thinking in the world market-place, and when identical opinions are expressed from so many countries they undoubtedly help to confirm the picture of English emerging as a global language.

Communications

If a language is a truly international medium, it is going to be most apparent in those services which deal directly with the task of communication – the postal and telephone systems and the electronic networks. Information about the use of English in these domains is not easy to come by, however. No one monitors the language in which we write our letters; there is no-one noting the language we use when we talk on the phone. Only on the Internet, where messages and data can be left for indefinite periods of time, is it possible to develop an idea of how much of the world's everyday communications (at least, between computer-owners) is actually in English.

There are various indirect methods of calculation, of course. We can draw up a list of those countries where English has special status (see chapter 2), and look at the pieces of mail sent, or the number of telephone calls made. Data of this kind are available, though hedged in with many qualifications. For example, using the information compiled in the 1995 Britannica

Yearbook, it transpires that about 60 per cent of the world's mail in 1992 was being handled by English-status countries. However, information is not available for forty-five countries, and those countries which have provided totals arrived at them in a variety of ways.

One fact is plain: the amount of mail sent through just the US postal system that year (some 165 thousand million pieces) was larger than the total for all the non-English-speaking countries put together. Indeed, if the USA is matched against **all** other countries, it accounts for nearly half of the world's volume of postal traffic. Even if we assume that the proportion of the US population which speaks other languages (about 15 per cent) never writes in English, we must still conclude that 40 per cent of the world's mail is in English, from the USA alone.

A widely quoted statistic is that three-quarters of the world's mail is in English. It is certainly possible to arrive at this figure if we make guesses about the number of people in different countries who are involved in organizations which use English as an official language, or which rely on English for correspondence. When scientists from any country write to each other, for example, the language they use is almost always going to be English. The figures for international mail are likely to reflect those for international associations cited above, where again English is widespread. But there are no precise calculations.

Another widely quoted statistic is that about 80 per cent of the world's electronically stored information is currently in English. Figures of this kind relate to two kinds of data: information stored privately by individual firms and organizations, such as commercial businesses, libraries and security forces; and information made available through the Internet, whether for sending and receiving electronic mail, participating in discussion groups, or providing and accessing databases and data pages. Statistics of this kind have to be cautiously interpreted. They seem to be little more than extrapolations from computer sales and distribution patterns – and thus simply reflect the pioneering role of the USA in developing and marketing computational hardware and software. In particular, given the American origins of the Internet (as ARPANET, the Advanced Research Projects Agency network devised in the late 1960s), it is not surprising that most Internet hosts – 64 per cent, according to a *Business Week* survey in April 1996 – are to be found in the USA. A further 12.7 per cent were thought to be in other English-speaking countries. But there is no easy way of predicting the language of Internet users or documents from the location of their hosts.

It is important for the theme of this book to see how English came to have such a dominant position on the Internet. ARPANET was conceived as a decentralized national network, its aim being to link important American academic and government institutions in a way which would survive local damage in the event of a major war. Its language was, accordingly, English; and when people in other countries began to form links with this network, it proved essential for them to use English. The dominance of this language was then reinforced when the service was opened up in the 1980s to private and commercial organizations, most of which were (for the reasons given earlier in this chapter) already communicating chiefly in English.

There was also a technical reason underpinning the position of the language at this time. The first protocols devised to carry data on the Net were developed for the English alphabet, using a character set (called Latin 1) which had no diacritical marks and which was transmitted in a 7-bit ASCII code. An 8-bit code and a character set including diacritics (Latin 2) later became available, and more sophisticated protocols were devised with multilingualism in mind, but major problems have hindered their international implementation in a standardized way. There are problems of data representation and manipulation (especially involving the selection, encoding, and conversion of character sets), data display (handling such issues as the direction of a writing system, or the mapping of character codes into an appropriate range of images on screen), and data input (such as the use of different keyboard layouts and techniques). Several *ad hoc* solutions have been devised, but *ad hoc* solutions bring with them problems of compatibility, and this limits the ability of the World Wide Web to be truly interoperable – that is, enabling all servers and clients to communicate intelligently with each other, whatever the data source.

Most browsers are still unable to handle multilingual data presentation. More than just diacritics is involved, as is evident from a consideration of such writing systems as Arabic, Chinese, Korean, Thai and Hindi, some of which require very large character sets. More than alphabetic text is involved: there are difficulties in handling conventions to do with money, dates, measurements, and other types of special setting which need to be anticipated. At present a truly multilingual World Wide Web remains a long-term goal – a Web where end users can expect to input data using their language of choice in a routine way, and can expect any server to receive and display the data without problems. The Babel site, an Alis Technologies/Internet Society joint project to internationalize the Internet, is a good source of information on current developments (http://babel.alis.com: 8080).

In the meantime, English continues to be the chief lingua franca of the Internet – a position which is now beginning to be acknowledged in the popular media. For example, in April 1996 *The New York Times* carried an article by Michael Specter headed 'World, Wide, Web: 3 English Words', in which the role of English was highlighted:

To study molecular genetics, all you need to get into the Harvard University Library, or the medical library at Sweden's Karolinska Institute, is a phone line and a computer.

And, it turns out, a solid command of the English language. Because whether you are a French intellectual pursuing the cutting edge of international film theory, a Japanese paleobotanist curious about a newly discovered set of primordial fossils, or an American teen-ager concerned about Magic Johnson's jump shot, the Internet and World Wide Web really only work as great unifiers if you speak English.

Specter concludes: 'if you want to take full advantage of the Internet there is only one way to do it: learn English, which has more than ever become America's greatest and most effective export'. The article goes on to consider the international conse-quences of this situation – and in particular some of the negative ones. A sub-heading reads: 'A force for global unity' – adding in ironic parentheses '(if you know the language)'. Specter quotes

Anatoly Voronov, the director of Glasnet, an Internet provider in Russia:

It is the ultimate act of intellectual colonialism. The product comes from America so we must either adapt to English or stop using it. That is the right of business. But if you are talking about a technology that is supposed to open the world to hundreds of millions of people you are joking. This just makes the world into new sorts of haves and have nots.

Is it a serious possibility – that unless you are able to use English, you will be unable to take advantage of the intellectual power which the Internet provides? Does the Net have the power to divide people into two classes of citizen – Internet literates and illiterates? Is the 'intellectual ghetto' a real prospect?

The problem seems large now, but it is probably only temporary. Anatoly Voronov comments that 'it is far easier for a Russian language speaker with a computer to download the works of Dostoyevsky translated into English to read than it is for him to get the original in his own language'. This is a pity. But the speed with which the Net is growing and adapting is so great that it is unlikely that the situation will obtain for long. Eventually, someone will find it worthwhile to put Dostoyevsky on the Net. It may well be happening already. As the demand for material in other languages grows, so will the supply. None of this will remove the dominance of English on the Net, but it will reduce the risk of international intellectual ghettoes. That risk, in any case, is less to do with linguistics than it is with economics, education, and technology: can people afford to buy computers? do they know how to use them? does their country have the necessary infrastructure? is finance available for database compilation? Computer illiteracy is more the result of lack of money than lack of English.

Although many people regret the current lack of their language's presence on the Internet, there are few who fail to see the value of having a lingua franca. A typical observation is that of a Polish commentator, Pavel Radkovsky, whose essay, 'English, the lingua franca of the Internet', was available on the Web in 1996. He asserts:

the expansion of the Internet strengthens the leading status of English. I can claim that many of those who have started learning or improving their English do so because they want to understand better what appeared on their computer screens after they had transferred packets of data from other computers. In other words, the more the network spreads, the more people are encouraged to learn English and the stronger the position of English becomes.

The view carries especial weight, coming as it does from someone who has learned English as a foreign language, and who even draws attention to the fact by elegantly apologising for his mistakes in English (few though they are) at the end of his essay.

Is it possible to provide evidence to test impressions of this kind about the strength of English? Can the 80 per cent claim referred to above be substantiated? One technique is to carry out a series of searches on a particular host to see how many of the items retrieved are in English. For example, a Netscape search made in July 1996 on the World Wide Web using Lycos established that all of the references made to *tritium* were in English – as we might expect for such an unequivocably scientific subject. A search for information about a cultural item, *orchestras*, found only one record in the first 100 documents in a language other than English. Interestingly, several orchestras from non-English-status countries had ensured that their Web page was in English – for example, the Shanghai National Music Orchestra (China) and the Lahti Symphony Orchestra (Finland). Also of interest was the corresponding search carried out on the word for *orchestra* in other languages: *orchestre* (French) produced 39 English entries out of the first 100; *Orchester* (German) produced 34 out of 76 (the total number of records found); and *orquestra* (Spanish) produced 35 out of 78. It is quite common to see a message attached to a foreign-language record: 'These pages are also available in English'. It is unusual to see the corresponding foreign-language message attached to an English page.

If we carry out a series of random searches in this way, for both English-language and other-language keywords, we do consistently end up with a figure of about 80 per cent. However, this comment relates to 1996: the proportion is going to become much less, as more people from more countries come on-line, and the changes are likely to be very rapid, in view of the remarkable growth in Internet use. From a million users in 1990, estimates by the Internet Society suggest there were 20 million users in 1993, and over 40 million by the end of 1995, with growth continuing at a rate of about 10 per cent a month in 1996. Web users at that time were represented in some 90 countries, and e-mail facilities were available in a further 70 countries. The number of non-English language users on the Internet is thus growing all the time, and is probably exceeding the number of new English-speaking users. In particular, minority languages are finding that the Net gives them a louder and cheaper voice than is available through such traditional media as radio, and Usenet groups are now ongoing in, for example, Galician, Basque, Irish, Breton and Welsh. Well over 100 languages routinely use the Internet in this way, notwithstanding the technical difficulties referred to above. This is good news for those worried by the global trend in language loss (p. 17), but it is also good news for those concerned that global intelligibility should not lose out to local identity. On the Net, all languages are as equal as their users wish to make them, and English emerges as an alternative rather than a threat.

The right place at the right time

What are we to conclude, after this wideranging review of the way English has come to be used in the modern world? Is there a common theme which can help us explain the remarkable growth of this language? The evidence of this chapter, and that of chapter 3, is that it is a language which has repeatedly found itself in the right place at the right time.

In the seventeenth and eighteenth centuries English was the language of the leading colonial nation – Britain. In the eighteenth and nineteenth centuries it was the language of the leader of the industrial revolution – also Britain. In the late-nineteenth century and the early twentieth it was the language of the leading economic power – the USA. As a result, when new technologies brought new linguistic opportunities, English emerged as a first-rank language in industries which affected all aspects of society – the press, advertising, broadcasting, motion pictures, sound recording, transport and communications. At the same time, the world was forging fresh networks of international alliances, and there emerged an unprecedented need for a lingua franca. Here too, there was a clear first choice. During the first half of the twentieth century English gradually became a leading language of international political, academic, and community meetings.

By the 1960s, the pre-eminence of the language was established, but it could not at that time have been described as a genuine world language, in the sense described in chapter 1. Since then, however, two events have together ensured its global status. The first was the movement towards political independence, out of which English emerged as a language with special status in several new countries. In most of these, the role of English had come to be so fundamental that no other language could compete, when the moment of independence arrived. The other event was the electronic revolution, where here too English was in the right place (the USA) at the right time (the 1970s).

The development of twentieth-century computers has been almost entirely an American affair. as Michael Specter puts it, in his *New York Times* article: 'The Internet started in the United States, and the computer hackers whose reality has always been virtual are almost all Americans. By the time the net spread, its linguistic patterns – like its principal architecture and best software – were all Made in the USA.' Although computer languages are not like natural languages, being very restricted, they have inevitably been greatly influenced by the mother tongue of the programmers – and this has largely been English. The first computer operating systems automatically used English vocabulary and syntax, as can be seen in such instructions as 'Press any key when ready' and 'Volume in Drive B has no label'. These are examples from MS (Microsoft) DOS, the system developed in 1977 by US computer entrepreneur Bill Gates, and which was adopted by IBM in 1981 for its range of computers. It is thought that there are now over 115 million computers in use throughout the world, with IBM the clear market leader. The more recent operating systems, replacing DOS, have displayed

English influence too, though alternatives in a few other languages are now available (where the commercial advantages have justified the development costs, as in French and German). And it seems likely that the influence of English will grow, as programs become increasingly sophisticated and allow users to make more natural-sounding commands.

It is difficult to predict the future, with something so dynamic as the Internet. In a few generations' time, the Net will not be like anything we know today. Automatic speech synthesis and recognition will be routine, and (notwithstanding the difficulties described on p. 21) more use will be made of automatic translation. For the immediate future, it is difficult to foresee any developments which could seriously reduce the stature of English on the information superhighway. The biggest potential setback to English as a global language, it has been said with more than a little irony, would have taken place a generation ago – if Bill Gates had grown up speaking Chinese.

5

The future of global English

After a while, any account of the social history of English, such as the one recounted in chapters 3 and 4, starts to repeat itself. Under each heading, the narrative identifies a major domain of modern society, puts it in a historical perspective, then discusses the extent to which it now uses or depends upon English. The overwhelming impression, after such an exercise, must be that the language is alive and well, and that its global future is assured.

But linguistic history shows us repeatedly that it is wise to be cautious, when making predictions about the future of a language. If, in the Middle Ages, you had dared to predict the death of Latin as the language of education, people would have laughed in your face – as they would, in the eighteenth century, if you had suggested that any language other than French could be a future norm of polite society. A week may be a long time in politics; but a century is a short time in linguistics.

In speculating about the future of English as a world language, therefore, we need to pay careful attention to indications which seem to go against the general trend. And we need to ask, in broad terms: What kinds of development could impede the future growth of English? It will then be possible to arrive at a balanced conclusion.

113

The rejection of English

We begin with the situation where the people of a country feel so antagonistic or ambivalent about English that they reject the option to give English a privileged status, either as an official language or as a foreign language. If several countries were to begin thinking in this way, there could in due course be a pendulum swing which would render the claim of global status less credible. The chief reasons for such antipathy were briefly discussed in chapter 1, when we began our inquiry into the general nature of a global language. We may apply this reasoning now, in relation to the particular case of English.

It is inevitable that, in a post-colonial era, there should be a strong reaction against continuing to use the language of the former colonial power, and in favour of promoting the indigenous languages. As the then president of Kenya, Jomo Kenyatta, said in 1974, 'The basis of any independent government is a national language, and we can no longer continue aping our former colonizers.' Gandhi, writing in 1908, puts the point more emotively:

To give millions a knowledge of English is to enslave them . . . Is it not a painful thing that, if I want to go to a court of justice, I must employ the English language as a medium; that, when I became a Barrister, I may not speak my mother-tongue, and that someone else should have to translate to me from my own language? Is this not absolutely absurd? Is it not a sign of slavery?

The Kenyan author, Ngugi wa Thiong'o, who chose to reject English as the medium of expression for his work in favour of Gikuyu and Kiswahili, is equally forceful in his book *Decolonising the Mind* (1986):

I am lamenting a neo-colonial situation which has meant the European bourgeoisie once again stealing our talents and geniuses as they have stolen our economies. In the eighteenth and nineteenth centuries Europe stole art treasures from Africa to decorate their houses and museums; in the twentieth century Europe is stealing the treasures of the mind to enrich their languages and cultures. Africa needs back its economy, its politics, its culture, its languages and all its patriotic writers.

114

The arguments are all to do with identity, and with language as the most immediate and universal symbol of that identity. People have a natural wish to use their own mother-tongue, to see it survive and grow, and they do not take kindly when the language of another culture is imposed on them. Despite the acknowledged values which the language of that culture can bring, the fact remains that English has an unhappy colonial resonance in the minds of many, and a history where local languages could easily be treated with contempt. Here is another extract from *Decolonising the Mind*, in which Ngugi wa Thiong'o remembers his schooldays:

English became the language of my formal education. In Kenya, English became more than a language: it was *the* language, and all the others had to bow before it in deference. Thus one of the most humiliating experiences was to be caught speaking Gikuyu in the vicinity of the school. The culprit was given corporal punishment – three to five strokes of the cane on bare buttocks – or was made to carry a metal plate around the neck with inscriptions such as I AM STUPID or I AM A DONKEY.

It is not difficult to see how antagonism to English can grow, with such memories. Equally, it is easy to see how ambivalence can grow. Many writers in the countries of the outer circle see themselves as facing a dilemma: if they write in English, their work will have the chance of reaching a worldwide audience; but to write in English may mean sacrificing their cultural identity.

On the whole, the former colonies of the British Empire have stayed with English (see the list at the end of chapter 2), but there are some famous instances of rejection. These are Tanzania, where English was jointly official with Swahili until 1967 (thereafter, Swahili became the sole official language); Kenya, where in 1974 English was officially replaced by Swahili; and Malaysia, where the National Language Act of 1967 disestablished English as a joint official language, giving sole status to Malay. On the other hand, English has begun to increase its prestige in several countries which were formerly part of other empires, and where it has no unpalatable colonial associations. In 1996, for example, Algeria (a former French colony) opted to make English its chief foreign language in schools, replacing French. And it is interesting to note that, in the excited debates surrounding the proposed creation of the state of Padania in Northern Italy, also in 1996, some secessionists were citing English as a more acceptable candidate for a lingua franca than standard Italian.

There are also economic arguments which might persuade a country to reduce its investment in the English language. A country might see its economic future as operating more on a regional than a global level, and thus devote extra resources to fostering a local lingua franca. The Spanish-speaking countries of Latin America could throw their weight behind Spanish, for example, or the countries of North Africa behind Arabic. Hindi, Russian, and German are other examples of languages which have a traditional presence within a number of geographically adjacent countries. The immediate benefits of using a language already well established in the locality could outweigh, in their mind, the longer-term benefits of introducing English. They might want no part in a global economic village, or dismiss the possibility as a pipe-dream. The current debate on the merits and demerits of European economic union suggests that the benefits are not always clear.

The need for intelligibility and the need for identity often pull people – and countries – in opposing directions. The former motivates the learning of an international language, with English the first choice in most cases; the latter motivates the promotion of ethnic language and culture. Conflict is the common consequence when either position is promoted insensitively. There are ways of avoiding such conflict, of course, notably in the promotion of bilingual or multilingual policies, which enable people both 'to have their cake and eat it'. But bilingual policies are expensive to resource, in both time and money, and they require a climate of cooperation which for historical reasons often does not exist.

Any decision to reject English has important consequences for the identity of a nation, and it can cause emotional ripples (both sympathetic and antagonistic) around the English-speaking world; but there have been very few such rejections of English to date, and the populations in the countries which have done so are sufficiently small that even in total there has been no noticeable impact on the status of the English language as a whole. There is, however, one country where, on grounds of population-size alone, a major change in the sociolinguistic situation could turn ripples into waves. That is the USA.

The US situation

Given that the USA has come to be the dominant element in so many of the domains identified in earlier chapters, the future status of English must be bound up to some extent with the future of that country. So much of the power which has fuelled the growth of the English language during the twentieth century has stemmed from America. We have already noted that the country contains nearly four times as many mother-tongue speakers of English as any other nation. It has been more involved with international developments in twentieth-century technology than any other nation. It is in control of the new industrial (that is, electronic) revolution. And it exercises a greater influence on the way English is developing worldwide than does any other regional variety – often, of course, to the discomfiture of people in the UK, Australia, New Zealand, Canada and South Africa, who regularly express worries in their national presses about the onslaught of 'Americanisms'.

As we have seen in chapter 1, there is the closest of links between language and power. If anything were to disestablish the military or economic power of the USA, there would be inevitable consequences for the global status of the language. The millions of people learning English in order to have access to this power would begin to look elsewhere, and (assuming the new political magnet used a language other than English) they would quickly acquire new language loyalties. It is unlikely that a corresponding loss of power in any other country would have such a serious effect. Even if, for example, the entire English-speaking population of Canada decided to switch to French, or the entire English-speaking population of South Africa opted to speak Afrikaans, the implications for English as a world language would be minor. As can be seen from the listing in chapter 2, relatively small numbers of people would be involved.

No one has suggested that the power of the USA is seriously at risk from external forces, as we approach the new millennium; the International Institute for Strategic Studies (in *The Military Balance 1996–7*) reports that the USA still has by far the most powerful conventional armed forces in the world and is the largest arms producer. But during the past decade increasing attention has come to be focused on a domestic debate in which, according to one set of arguments, there are internal forces threatening the country's future unity. As we have seen in chapter 2 (p. 31), some analysts consider the English language to have been an important factor in maintaining mutual intelligibility and American unity in the face of the immigration explosion which more than tripled the US population after 1900. For those who take this view, the contemporary movement among some immigrant populations to maintain their original cultural identity through safeguarding their mother tongues is – given the large numbers involved – a matter of some consequence. What has emerged is a conflict between the demands of intelligibility and identity (of the kind outlined in chapter 1), and one outcome has been the 'official English' movement. Although the various arguments are in many ways unique to the USA, given the large numbers of people and languages involved, and relating as they do to the rights of individuals as enshrined in the US Constitution, they need to be carefully noted by people in other countries, for ethnic minority and immigrant populations – and thus the competing pressures of identity preservation vs. assimilation – are everywhere. Although there is no official-language movement in Britain, for example, it is not impossible to imagine an analogous situation developing there, as well as in Australia, where immigration trends in recent years have been especially dramatic, and where in 1996 the country's attitude towards Asian immigrants emerged again as a political issue. A summary of the main issues is therefore of some relevance, in a book dealing with the future of global English.

Why, in a country where 95 per cent or so of the population speak English, should there be a movement to make English official? People do not start making a case for a language to be made official until they feel they need to; and the circumstances in which they need to are usually very clear. The typical scenario is one where a language needs to be protected because its existence is threatened by the emergence of a more dominant language. In such cases, the dominant power may take measures to preserve it (usually, after forceful pressure from the members of the minority community) by giving it special recognition. This has happened occasionally, and especially in recent decades, among the countries of the inner circle (p. 54): for example, some degree of official status has now been given to Welsh in Wales, Irish Gaelic in Ireland, French in Quebec, Hawaiian in the Hawaii Islands, and Maori in New Zealand. And in each case, it has proved necessary to pay attention to the corresponding official role of English, in these territories, also as a protective measure. But in a country where the language is already so dominant, and its position for so long taken for granted (p. 75), why should the question of its official status arise at all?

Before going into the reasons, it should be mentioned that the positions for and against 'official English' have been argued with varying amounts of moderation and extremism, and that several views are possible on each side. On the pro-official side, no less than three bills came before the House of Representatives in January–February 1995, all sponsored by Republicans (but with varying amounts of inter-party support), expressing different attitudes and recommendations about the use and status of other languages. The most moderate of these (HR 123, sponsored by Representative Bill Emerson), outlined below, saw itself partly as a means of empowering immigrants by giving them greater opportunities to acquire English. Considerably more radical was HR 739, sponsored by Representative Toby Roth, which allowed for fewer exceptions in the official use of other languages, and repealed the 1965 Act providing for bilingual education and bilingual ballots. More restrictive still was HR 1005, sponsored by Representative Pete King, which allowed for even fewer exceptions in the use of other languages. The latter two proposals made little political progress; but HR 123 received the support of US English, the country's leading organization campaigning for official English, and it was this bill which eventually went to a vote, in August 1996, being passed by the

House of Representatives (under the name of the Bill Emerson English Language Empowerment Act) by 259 to 169. However, pressure of time in a presidential election year did not allow the bill to reach the Senate, and it remains to be seen how the issue will fare in the next Congress.

This summary of the main clauses of the Emerson bill is based on the bill as presented to the House on 4 January 1995. It does not include any amendments introduced at the committee stage in July 1996 or thereafter.

(1) the United States is comprised of individuals and groups from diverse ethnic, cultural, and linguistic backgrounds;

(2) the United States has benefited and continues to benefit from this rich diversity;

(3) throughout the history of the Nation, the common thread binding those of differing backgrounds has been a common language;

(4) in order to preserve unity in diversity, and to prevent division along linguistic lines, the United States should maintain a language common to all people;

(5) English has historically been the common language and the language of opportunity in the United States;

(6) the purpose of this Act is to help immigrants better assimilate and take full advantage of economic and occupational opportunities in the United States;

(7) by learning the English language, immigrants will be empowered with the language skills and literacy necessary to become responsible citizens and productive workers in the United States;

(8) the use of a single common language in the conduct of the Government's official business will promote efficiency and fairness to all people;

(9) English should be recognized in law as the language of official business of the Government; and

(10) any monetary savings derived from the enactment of this Act should be used for the teaching of non-English speaking immigrants the English language.

In a series of further clauses, it was made clear that 'official business' meant 'those governmental actions, documents, or policies which are enforceable with the full weight and authority of the Government' – this would include all public records, legislation, regulations, hearings, official ceremonies, and public meetings. The bill allowed the use of languages other than English in such cases as public health and safety services, the teaching of foreign languages, policies necessary for international relations and trade, and actions that protect the rights of people involved in judicial proceedings. Private businesses were not affected. The bill also stated that it was not its purpose 'to discriminate against or restrict the rights of any individual' or 'to discourage or prevent the use of languages other than English in any nonofficial capacity'.

There are also several positions on the anti-official side, though here it is not so easy to make generalizations. To begin with, there are many cultural perspectives, as we would expect from a population which includes, on the one hand, a major Hispanic group of over 17 millions (according to the 1990 census) and, on the other, a range of ethnic groups whose members number only a few thousand. No less than 329 languages were in regular use, at the time of that census. Also, there is no single authoritative source of statement to refer to, but many organizations, each of which has its own political agenda. The observations below, accordingly, will not necessarily be held by everyone who opposes official English legislation. They are paraphrases of views expressed in various policy statements, alternative proposals, and press articles or letters. But the points can be used in aggregate to spell out the case for opposition.

A wide range of arguments is used by each side in support of its case.

- *The political argument: for* Pro-official supporters see in the emergence of major immigrant groups, and the support for immigrant language programmes, the seeds of separatism, and the eventual dissolution of the unity which is reflected in the very name of the United States and its motto (*E pluribus unum*, 'One out of many'). They look fearfully at the language-inspired separatist movement in nearby Quebec, which came close to success in 1995, and draw attention to the emergence of incendiary separatist attitudes such as are expressed by the Chicano Movement of Aztlan (MECha) or by the University of

California student publication, *Voz Fronteriza* ('Voice of the Frontier'), where writers envisage large tracts of the US south-west as one day returning to Hispanic (Mexicano) control. The term 'official Spanish' is increasingly encountered, in this connection. The fact that there is a linguistic dimension to the conflicts which destroyed former Yugoslavia is also sometimes cited as an example of the dangers lurking beneath the surface of a multilingual community: Speaker of the House Newt Gingrich, for example, participating in the debate on the Emerson bill, was one influential voice which referred to the perils of US 'Balkanization'.

From this point of view, English is viewed, according to one pro-official columnist in 1995, as a social adhesive – as a linguistic glue which guarantees political unity. According to another, the language has been the basis of social stability in the USA, and any threat to this stabilizing influence would lead to the growth of 'countries within a country' – linguistic ghettos which would discourage contact between groups and slow down the process of socialization. Attention is drawn to the size of the possible rift, especially in relation to the use of Spanish, with the US Census Bureau predicting more Hispanics than African-Americans in the USA by the year 2010, and a Hispanic population of over 80 million by 2050.

• *The political argument: against* Anti-official supporters maintain that an official English bill is unnecessary – that the fears have been wildly exaggerated, there is no risk of disunity, and no danger of Babel. They argue that most immigrants are assimilating nicely – certainly by the second generation – and that the natural course of events will eventually produce a new social balance, without any need for legislation. There is no more need to make English official now, it is suggested, than there was at the time of the Revolution, when Dutch and German were for a while spoken by substantial numbers. The natural urge that people have to succeed will provide the required motivation for the learning of English. A common observation, they point out, is that first-generation immigrant parents actually find it harder to persuade their children to learn their language of origin than to learn

English. It is felt that English could not possibly be in danger, in any case, when over 95 per cent of the population speak it 'well' or 'very well' (according to the 1990 census). It is the other languages which are actually in danger.

Many accordingly hold the view that the official English bill is an unwarranted federal intrusion into self-expression, violating cultural pluralism, and – insofar as it is perceived as a policy intended to limit and control minorities – increasing the chances that communities would divide along ethnic lines. Even if English were made official, the argument continues, the use of a common language does not guarantee ethnic harmony. A community can be torn apart on racial, religious, political, or other grounds, even when both sides are united by a single language (see p. 13). There are evidently bigger issues in the world than linguistic ones, and this is reflected in some of the descriptors used by those most violently opposed to the 'official English' proposals, such as 'elitist', 'racist', 'anti-immigrant' and 'anti-Hispanic'.

• *The socio-economic argument: for* Pro-official supporters maintain that, at a time when there is considerable competition for limited funds, an expensive multilingual support policy is undesirable. It is not as if there is just a single alternative language which is in need of protection (as in the case of Canada): there are well over 300 languages to be taken into account. They point out that no country could afford a language policy which tried to give official protection to so many languages. The Canadian situation, dealing with just two languages, cost that country nearly $7,000 million dollars in the decade from 1980 to 1990. The USA, with ten times the population, and many more languages, would have to find some multiple of that total each year, depending on how many languages were selected for support.

The problem of selection is thought to be particularly serious. Pro-official supporters draw attention to the difficulty of saying that a language can receive official recognition only after it reaches a certain point of growth. If 5 million were chosen as the cut-off point, for example, it would be inevitable that people who spoke languages which were just a little short of that figure would claim that the division was unfair. Some commentators therefore argue that no principled selection is possible, and that the country is in an all-or-none situation. If 'all': any foreign-language groups with a tiny number of speakers would be able to claim official support – but the country would soon go bankrupt, if it adopted such a policy. The only alternative, this line of argument concludes, is to support 'none' – other than the language of the vast majority, English.

It is also argued that the provision of alternative language services (such as the option of taking a driving test in a range of different languages) is highly wasteful of resources, because they are so little used. One of the main themes of the leading pro-English organization in the USA, US English, is to draw attention to cases of this kind. For example, it cites the fact that in 1994 the Internal Revenue Service distributed half a million forms and instruction booklets in Spanish, but only 718 were returned. It expresses concern about the cost of a language policy in which, for instance, in 1996 California was offering licence exams to drivers in thirty-five different languages. It concludes that a better return for money would come from spending it elsewhere: in improving the English-language abilities of immigrants to the USA. There is an important issue of empowerment here: pro-official supporters argue that edu-cational programmes in the immigrant's mother tongue are no real help, because they eliminate the incentive for immigrants to learn English, and this keeps them in low-paid jobs. Official status, it is asserted, would help to safeguard English as the language of opportunity. There would also be enormous savings in efficiency, both at national and local levels, it is suggested, if everyone had the competence and confidence to rely on English as their medium of communication in official contexts. This would also ensure that everyone would understand road signs, safety regulations at work, medicinal instructions, environmental hazard warnings, and the like. If it is possible for someone to have such a poor knowledge of English that they have to take a driving exam in another language, the argument concludes, it is improb-able that they will be able to cope with the English-language demands placed upon them by the multiplicity of road-side instructions.

• *The socio-economic argument: against*   Anti-official supporters doubt whether government time and money would really be saved, given the cost and complexity of introducing the new law. In particular, they question whether the legislation could possibly be enforced, and point to the difficulties of giving a precise definition to the notion of 'official', in relation to language, and of making a clear and consistent distinction between 'public' and 'private' discourse. For example, would a march in support of some minority issue be a public or private event, and would it be permitted to carry banners in languages other than English? The fear is that the public domain will gradually erode the private one, ultimately threatening freedom of speech. Especially in a country where there is a great readiness to use the courts to solve disputes, the new law would, it is felt, cause greater complications than it would solve, and would probably be more expensive to implement and maintain. It might actually end up being honoured more in the breach than in the observance, with the legislation proving inadequate to cope with the realities of a highly complex and dynamic social situation. An important complication is that any new layer of federal control would also have to be implemented alongside the individual laws enacted by several states (twenty-three by 1996), which already display a great deal of variation.

The 'all-or-nothing' view of language support is also hotly contested, using the following line of reasoning. There may indeed be no principled way of drawing a line between one group of languages and another, but it does not follow from this that nothing should be done to help those who speak the more widely used languages, where relatively large numbers of people would benefit from receiving a modicum of support in their mother tongue. The fields of health and safety, such as those cited above, provide a good example of areas where much more could be done than is available at present. Some commentators have drawn attention to the different situation in other countries which have high immigrant populations. In Germany, for example, pharma-ceutical companies have to provide instruction labels in five *Gastarbeiter* (immigrant 'guest-worker') languages: Turkish,

Italian, Spanish, Serbo-Croatian, and Greek. They are not
required to carry such labels in the several other languages
currently found in Germany, such as Russian and Polish. In this
view, to introduce a policy banning all such labels on the grounds
that some languages cannot be represented is felt to be absurd. It
is thought to be common sense to provide safety instructions
on medicine bottles in as many languages as is practicable, to
minimize the risk to as many people as possible. It is not feasible
to help everyone who has difficulty with English, but it is not
acceptable to conclude from this that the government should
therefore help none of them.

Even though the moderate official-English position maintains
that it has no intention of harming ethnic identity or the natural
growth of languages other than English, anti-official supporters
claim that the withdrawal of resources and the fresh focus on
English is bound to harm the provision of services in these
languages, even in areas which are supposed to be protected, such
as health care and law enforcement. It is also thought likely that
interest in foreign-language learning will further diminish, and
this is felt to be an unfortunate development at a time when the
climate in international business competitiveness and political
diplomacy is one where foreign-language ability is increasingly
seen as advantageous (see p. 16).

• *Educational issues* Several other kinds of argument are used
in the debate – in particular, to do with educational theory and
practice. For example, the pro-official position is concerned that
many students in bilingual education programmes are being
taught by teachers whose own level of English is of a low quality,
thus inculcating an inadequate command of the language, and a
'ghetto dialect' that will mark the speakers as socially inferior.
They point to the shortage of adequately trained teachers, and to
the many problems in assigning students to the right kind of
programme for the right length of time, and claim that bilingual
programmes are not as efficient as English-immersion programmes in fostering the transition to mainstream English
classes. Anti-official supporters stress the value of bilingualism as
part of a child's learning experience, observing that immigrant

children are more likely to do well in learning a second language if their own language is valued by the society in which they find themselves. They stress the potential for success of bilingual education programmes, arguing that the best predictor of achievement in English for immigrant children by age eighteen is the amount of time spent in bilingual classrooms. If there are inadequacies in the educational system, it is suggested, these are due to the failure of government to provide enough financial support for learning resources, educational facilities, and teacher training, and to the fact that bilingual programmes are available to only about 25 per cent of students with limited English proficiency. The 'official English' bill, it is pointed out, does virtually nothing to enable fluency in English to be be universally achieved – other than simply stating that it must be. To evaluate the arguments on both sides would require a detailed consideration of such matters as teaching methods, research procedures, and assessment goals, and is too complex an area to be given summary treatment in the present book. But it is important to appreciate that a great deal of time has been, and continues to be, devoted to this issue.

Many of those who support the pro-official position feel that the pendulum has swung too far in the wrong direction. From a position where transitional programmes were being devised to get children into the English-speaking mainstream as quickly as possible, they now see a position where these programmes are being used to preserve cultural identity and to reduce integration. From a position where immigrants were expected to learn English, they note cases of non-immigrants in schools now having to learn the immigrant language. From a position where English was the language an immigrant needed for a job, they now note cases where a monolingual English person would have to learn an immigrant language in order to be eligible for a job. They fear a society in which people will be appointed first for linguistic reasons, and only secondly for their other abilities and experience. These fears are by no means unique to the USA, of course. They surface wherever a bilingual policy is in operation. But they are expressed with special strength in the USA, partly because of the large numbers involved, and partly because the democratic tradition is so strongly supportive of the rights of the individual.

Many anti-official supporters, unconvinced by the pro-official arguments, find that there is no alternative but to conclude that the 'official English' position is one of (consciously or unconsciously held) elitism or discrimination. Minority languages are not being protected, in their view, but restricted. An 'official English' law, according to an alternative proposal which was formulated (the 'English Plus Resolution', introduced in the House in July 1995 by Representative Jose Serrano), would be 'an unwarranted Federal regulation of self-expression' and would 'abrogate constitutional rights to freedom of expression and equal protection of the laws'. It would also 'contradict the spirit of the 1923 Supreme Court case Meyer v. Nebraska, wherein the Court declared that "The protection of the Constitution extends to all; to those who speak other languages as well as to those born with English on the tongue".' To disregard this tradition of thinking, it was argued, could make a difficult social situation still more difficult. The Serrano bill claimed that official English legislation would 'violate traditions of cultural pluralism' and 'divide communities along ethnic lines'. By contrast, multilingualism could bring benefits to a community, helping to promote empathy between different ethnic groups. The leading linguistics organization of the USA, the Linguistic Society of America, in 1995 issued a statement on language rights whose final paragraph summarized the tenor of this approach:

Notwithstanding the multilingual history of the United States, the role of English as our common language has never seriously been questioned. Research has shown that newcomers to America continue to learn English at rates comparable to previous generations of immigrants. All levels of government should adequately fund programs to teach English to any resident who desires to learn it. Nonetheless, promoting our common language need not, and should not, come at the cost of violating the rights of linguistic minorities.

The 'English Plus Resolution' began by recognizing English as 'the primary language of the United States' alongside the importance of other languages spoken by US residents, and asserted that 'these linguistic resources should be conserved and developed'. It repeatedly stressed the value of multilingualism to the US community: this would 'enhance American competitiveness in global markets', 'improve United States diplomatic efforts by fostering enhanced communication and greater understanding between nations', and 'promote greater cross-cultural understanding between different racial and ethnic groups'. It recommended that the US government should pursue policies that:

(1) encourage all residents of this country to become fully proficient in English by expanding educational opportunities;
(2) conserve and develop the Nation's linguistic resources by encouraging all residents of this country to learn or maintain skills in a language other than English;
(3) assist native Americans, Native Alaskans, Native Hawaiians, and other peoples indigenous to the United States, in their efforts to prevent the extinction of their languages and cultures;
(4) continue to provide services in languages other than English as needed to facilitate access to essential functions of government, promote public health and safety, ensure due process, promote equal educational opportunity, and protect fundamental rights, and
(5) recognize the importance of multilingualism to vital American interests and individual rights, and oppose 'English-only' measures and similar language restrictionist measures.

However, the Serrano bill made no further progress in 1996, with political attention eventually focusing exclusively on the Emerson proposal (p. 120).

By the end of 1996, the future direction of the 'official English' debate was still unsettled. The language arguments had become increasingly polarized, and forced into line with the party politics of an election year; and the emotional level of the debate had escalated. There seems to be something about the intimate relationship between language, thought, individuality, and social identity which generates strong emotions. And in a climate where supporters of official English (no matter how moderate) have come to be routinely labelled 'racist', and immigrants wishing to use their own language (no matter how cultured) are castigated by such names as 'welfare hogs', it is difficult to see the grounds for compromise.

New Englishes

Salman Rushdie comments, in an essay called 'Commonwealth literature does not exist' (published in *Imaginary Homelands*), that 'the English language ceased to be the sole possession of the English some time ago'. Indeed, when even the largest English-speaking nation, the USA, turns out to have only about 20 per cent of the world's English speakers (as we saw in chapter 2), it is plain that no one can now claim sole ownership. This is probably the best way of defining a genuinely global language, in fact: that its usage is not restricted by countries or (as in the case of some artificial languages) by governing bodies.

The loss of ownership is of course uncomfortable to those, especially in Britain, who feel that the language is theirs by historical right; but they have no alternative. There is no way in which any kind of regional social movement, such as the purist societies which try to prevent language change or restore a past period of imagined linguistic excellence, can influence the global outcome. In the end, it comes down to population growth. In the list of English-speaking territories shown in chapter 2, the number of first-language (L1) speakers in the inner-circle countries is currently greater than the number of second-language (L2) English speakers in the outer-circle countries – if we take the higher estimates, 400 million, as opposed to 350 million. But the countries of the outer circle have, combined, a much greater growth rate than those of the inner circle: in 1995–6, an average of 2.3 per cent compared with 0.8 per cent. So, if current population and learning trends continue, this balance will soon change. Within ten years, there will certainly be more L2 speakers than L1 speakers. Within fifty years, there could be up to 50 per cent more. By that time, the only possible concept of ownership will be a global one.

An inevitable consequence of this development is that the language will become open to the winds of linguistic change in totally unpredictable ways. The spread of English around the world has already demonstrated this, in the emergence of new varieties of English in the different territories where the language has taken root. The change has become a major talking point only since the 1960s, hence the term by which these varieties are often known: 'new Englishes'. The different dialects of British and American English provide the most familiar example. These two varieties diverged almost as soon as the first settlers arrived in America. By the time Noah Webster was writing his dictionaries, there were hundreds of words which were known in the USA but not in Britain, pronunciation had begun to diverge quite markedly, and spellings were in the process of change. Today, there are thousands of differences between British and American English – two cultures, as Dylan Thomas once put it, 'separated by the barrier of a common language'.

Why do such differences emerge? In the case of the USA, a concern to develop a distinctive 'American standard' was prominent in Webster's thinking. He presented the case strongly in his *Dissertations on the English Language* (1789). It was partly a matter of honour 'as an independent nation . . . to have a system of our own, in language as well as government'. It was partly a matter of common sense, because in England 'the taste of her writers is already corrupted, and her language on the decline'. And it was partly a matter of practicality, England being at 'too great a distance to be our model'. This national or 'federal' language was inevitable, Webster thought, because the exploration of the new continent would bring many new words into the language, which Britain would not share; but it also needed fostering. Spelling reform, he concluded, would be a major step in that direction: 'a difference between the English orthography and the American . . . is an object of vast political consequence'. He was right. Language and political issues are always very closely connected, as we have seen in earlier chapters.

The forces which shaped the development of American English are many and various. They have been well summarized by US dialectologist Frederic G. Cassidy, in an essay on 'English in the United States' (1982):

The effect of the Revolution and of national independence was tremendous. No less a figure than Noah Webster saw here a great opportunity to cast off the 'corrupt' language of England and to rationalize and refine the language for the new nation. The attempt to found an academy for such a purpose, which had several times failed in Britain, was made once again under the leadership of Thomas Jefferson. But other forces were at work – popular forces – which were to have a powerful effect, especially when actual democracy, rather than limited upper-class governance, came to the fore under Andrew Jackson.

The surge of population westward, the phenomenon of the expanding frontier in which the restraints and standards of more settled society were thrown off, was reflected in the language. With little or no education, having to cope as best they could with harsh physical conditions, the 'conquerors of the West' became freely innovative in their language, ebullient with descriptive and metaphorical inventions – with 'tall talk', exaggerated humor, vigor that had no time for refinement.

In the East, in the cities, however, education flourished; the leading class had it and it became a national ideal: the mark of progress in any settlement was that a school had been started. Self-education, especially for talented people of humble beginnings, was widely practiced and admired. Public address, often learned in the 'school of hard knocks', carried to the people educational ideals and their kudos. Some of the interesting neologisms were the direct offspring of ignorance pretending to be learned. A whole school of humor portrayed its characters as unschooled but practically wise.

Cassidy is here thinking of the humour of such authors as Josh Billings, Artemus Ward, and other 'cracker-barrel philosophers' who delighted audiences and readers all over the USA in the late nineteenth century. 'Humin natur', comments Billings, in his homespun spelling, 'is the same all over the world, cept in Nu England, and thar its akordin tu sarcumstances.'

This kind of humorous writing cannot work unless people can see it is a joke – in other words, they must be able to recognize the spellings as non-standard, and be able to identify dialect grammar and vocabulary. Webster was sixty when Billings was born. Evidently, in quite a short time, American English had settled down in its new identity, and despite its dialect differences was capable of providing a unified, literary standard which the new nation was able to recognize and to which it could respond.

Many distinctive forms also identify the Englishes of the other countries of the inner circle: Australian English, New Zealand English, Canadian English, South African English, Caribbean English, and, within Britain, Irish, Scots, and Welsh English. Among the countries of the outer circle, several varieties have also grown in distinctiveness in recent decades, as we have seen in chapter 2. There is one group in India, Pakistan, Bangladesh, and Sri Lanka, often collectively called South Asian English. There is another group in the former British colonies in West Africa, and a further group in the former British colonies in East Africa. Other emerging varieties have been noted in the Caribbean and in parts of south-east Asia, such as Singapore.

The number of speakers involved in some of these new Englishes needs to be appreciated. In India, for example, the population has doubled since 1960, and is projected to pass a thousand million by the year 2000. It is thus the second most populous country in the world, after China, but its population growth rate is larger than China's (1.9 per cent in the early 1990s, as opposed to 1.3 per cent). There must now be approaching 50 million people in India who are competent in English. If current English-language learning trends continue (and with satellite television and other sources of English increasingly available, it looks as if they will increase), within the next generation there will be more speakers of English in India than there will be in Britain (where the growth rate is only 0.4 per cent).

These new Englishes are somewhat like the dialects we all recognize within our own country, except that they are on an international scale, applying to whole countries or regions. Instead of affecting mere thousands of speakers, as is typically the case with rural or urban regional dialects, they apply to millions. They are an inevitable consequence of the spread of English on a world scale. The study of language history shows that if two social groups come to be separated only by a mountain range or a wide river, they will soon begin to develop different habits of speech. It should not be surprising, then, to find new national dialects emerging when groups become separated by thousands of miles, and encounter totally different climates, fauna, and flora.

Dialects emerge because they give identity to the groups which

133

own them. If you wish to tell everyone which part of a country you are from, you can wave a flag, wear a label on your coat, or (the most convenient solution, because it is always with you) speak with a distinctive accent and dialect. Similarly, on the world stage, if you wish to tell everyone which country you belong to, an immediate and direct way of doing it is to speak in a distinctive way. These differences become especially noticeable in informal settings; for example, they are currently well represented in discussion groups on the Internet.

International varieties thus express national identities, and are a way of reducing the conflict between intelligibility and identity. Because a speaker from country A is using English, there is an intelligibility bond with an English speaker of country B – and this is reinforced by the existence of a common written language. On the other hand, because speaker A is not using exactly the same way of speaking as speaker B, both parties retain their identities. It is another way of 'having your cake and eating it'.

Will English fragment?

Inevitably, the emergence of new Englishes raises the spectre of fragmentation – the eventual dissolution of English into a range of mutually unintelligible languages (as happened when Latin gave rise to the various Romance languages, such as French, Spanish, and Italian, over 1,000 years ago). Prophets have been predicting such doom for some time. In 1877, the British philologist Henry Sweet (the probable model for Shaw's Henry Higgins in *Pygmalion/My Fair Lady*) thought that a century later 'England, America, and Australia will be speaking mutually unintelligible languages, owing to their independent changes of pronunciation'. The same point had been made nearly a century before by Noah Webster, in his *Dissertations* (1789). Webster thought that such a development would be 'necessary and unavoidable', and would result in 'a language in North America, as different from the future language of England, as the modern Dutch, Danish and Swedish are from the German, or from one another'. From Webster's pro-American point of view, of course, that would not have been such a bad thing.

Neither of these scholars proved to be accurate prophets. English has indeed developed new spoken varieties in the areas mentioned, but these are by no means mutually unintelligible. Difficulties of comprehension are sometimes encountered between speakers of inner-circle Englishes and those of outer-circle Englishes, especially when the parties talk quickly; but they can usually be quickly resolved, and they seem to be diminishing, partly because the availability of international television programmes via satellite is familiarizing everyone with the existence of other norms. Also, the continuing presence of standard written English, in the form of newspapers, textbooks, and other printed material, shows very little variation in the different English-speaking countries.

On the other hand, this whole topic is so recent that it is difficult to make predictions with much confidence. Many of the new varieties have grown extremely rapidly, so that it is difficult to establish their role in their society, or how people are reacting to them. In several cases, it is known that the rise of a local English generates controversy, within the community. Some writers seize on the new variety with enthusiasm, and try to make it even more distinctive. Others prefer to retain strong links with the British or American standard. Some teachers, likewise, allow the new forms into their teaching; others rule them out.

The Indian author Raja Rao, writing in 1963, was one who looked forward to the development of a new Indian English:

English is not really an alien language to us. It is the language of our intellectual make-up – like Sanskrit and Persian was before – but not of our emotional make-up . . . We cannot write like the English. We should not. We cannot write only as Indians. We have grown to look at the large world as part of us. Our method of expression has to be a dialect which will some day prove to be as distinctive and colourful as the Irish or the American.

And a similar view comes from Salman Rushdie, in the essay referred to above:

I don't think it is always necessary to take up the anti-colonial – or is it post-colonial? – cudgels against English. What seems to me to be happening is that those peoples who were once colonized by the language are now rapidly remaking it, domesticating it, becoming more and more relaxed about the way they use it. Assisted by the English language's enormous flexibility and size, they are carving out large territories for themselves within its front.

To take the case of India, only because it's the one in which I'm most familiar. The debate about the appropriateness of English in post-British India has been raging ever since 1947; but today, I find, it is a debate which has meaning only for the older generation. The children of independent India seem not to think of English as being irredeemably tainted by its colonial provenance. They use it as an Indian language, as one of the tools they have to hand.

The Nigerian novelist Chinua Achebe, in *Morning Yet on Creation Day* (1964), has made one of the clearest statements representing the middle-of-the-road position:

The price a world language must be prepared to pay is submission to many different kinds of use. The African writer should aim to use English in a way that brings out his message best without altering the language to the extent that its value as a medium of international exchange will be lost. He should aim at fashioning out an English which is at once universal and able to carry his peculiar experience . . . I feel that English will be able to carry the weight of my African experience. But it will have to be a new English, still in full communion with its ancestral home but altered to suit its new African surroundings.

In the years since these remarks were made, this is precisely what has been happening – and not only in Africa, but throughout the countries of the outer circle. There is even a suggestion that some of the territories of the expanding circle – those in which English is learned as a foreign language – may be bending English to suit their purposes. 'Euro-English' is a label sometimes given these days to the kind of English being used by French, Greek, and other diplomats in the corridors of power in the new European Union, for most of whom English is a foreign language. But in none of these cases is there any serious sign of the language breaking up into mutually unintelligible varieties.

Even if the new Englishes did become increasingly different, as years went by, the consequences for world English would not necessarily be fatal. A likely scenario is that our current ability to use more than one dialect would simply extend to meet the fresh demands of the international situation. A new form of English – let us think of it as 'World Standard Spoken English' (WSSE) – would almost certainly arise. Indeed, the foundation for such a development is already being laid around us.

Most people are already 'multidialectal' to a greater or lesser extent. They use one spoken dialect at home, when they are with their family or talking to other members of their local community: this tends to be an informal variety, full of casual pronunciation, colloquial grammar, and local turns of phrase. They use another spoken dialect when they are away from home, travelling to different parts of their country or interacting with others at their place of work: this tends to be a formal variety, full of careful pronunciation, conventional grammar, and standard vocabulary. Those who are literate have learned a third variety, that of written standard English which (apart from a few minor differences, such as British vs. American spelling) currently unites the English-speaking world.

In a future where there were many national Englishes, little would change. People would still have their dialects for use within their own country, but when the need came to communicate with people from other countries they would slip into WSSE. So, a multinational company might decide to hold a conference at which representatives from each of its country operations would be present. The reps from Calcutta, sharing a cab on their way to the conference, would be conversing in informal Indian English. The reps from Lagos, in their cab, would be talking in informal Nigerian English. The reps from Los Angeles would be using informal American English. Any one of these groups, overhearing any other, might well find the conversation difficult to follow. But when all meet at the conference table, there would be no problem: everyone would be using WSSE.

People who attend international conferences, or who write scripts for an international audience, or who are 'talking' on the Internet have probably already felt the pull of this new variety. It takes the form, for example, of consciously avoiding a word or phrase which you know is not going to be understood outside your own country, and of finding an alternative form of expression. It can also affect your pronunciation and grammar.

But it is too early to be definite about the way this variety will develop. WSSE is still in its infancy. Indeed, it has hardly yet been born.

Which variety will be most influential, in the development of WSSE? It seems likely that it will be US (rather than UK) English. The direction of influence has for some time been largely one-way. Many grammatical issues in contemporary British usage show the influence of US forms, US spellings are increasingly widespread (especially in computer contexts), and there is a greater passive awareness of distinctively US lexicon in the UK (because of media influence) than vice versa. On the other hand, the situation will be complicated by the emergence on the world scene of new linguistic features derived from the L2 varieties, which as we have seen will in due course become numerically dominant. No feature of L2 English has yet become a part of standard US or UK English; but, as the balance of speakers changes, there is no reason for L2 features not to become part of WSSE. This would be especially likely if there were features which were shared by several (or all) L2 varieties – such as the use of syllable-timed rhythm, or the widespread difficulty observed in the use of *th* sounds.

The development of WSSE can be predicted because it enables people, yet again, to 'have their cake and eat it'. The concept of WSSE does not replace a national dialect: it supplements it. People who can use both are in a much more powerful position than people who can use only one. They have a dialect in which they can continue to express their national identity; and they have a dialect which can guarantee international intelligibility, when they need it. The same dual tendencies can be seen on the Internet, incidentally, which simultaneously presents us with a range of informal identifying personal varieties and a corpus of universally intelligible standard English. It is an interesting context for those wishing to study the forces affecting language change, with users searching for a balance between the attraction of a 'cool', idiosyncratic, but often unintelligible linguistic persona and the need to use an 'uncool' standardized form of expression in order to make oneself understood!

'Having your cake and eating it', of course, also applies to the use of completely different languages as markers of identity. It may well be that the people travelling by cab to the international conference would be speaking Hindi, Hausa, and Spanish, respectively. When they all meet at the conference table, they would switch into WSSE. They do not have to give up their national linguistic identities just because they are going to an international meeting. But of course this scenario assumes that Hindi, Hausa, and Spanish are still respected, alive and well, and living in their respective home communities.

A unique event?

There has never been a language so widely spread or spoken by so many people as English. There are therefore no precedents to help us see what happens to a language when it achieves genuine world status; and predictions about the future, as we saw in the remarks of Noah Webster and Henry Sweet, have a habit of being wrong. The balance between the competing demands of intelligibility and identity is especially fragile, and can easily be affected by social change, such as a swing in immigrant policy, new political alliances, or a change in a country's population trends.

If we cannot predict the future, we can at least speculate, and there are some fascinating speculations to be made. It may well be the case, as was intimated earlier, that the English language has already grown to be independent of any form of social control. There may be a critical number or critical distribution of speakers (analogous to the notion of critical mass in nuclear physics) beyond which it proves impossible for any single group or alliance to stop its growth, or even influence its future. If there were to be a major social change in Britain which affected the use of English there, would this have any real effect on the world trend? It is unlikely. And, as we have seen, even the current chief player, the USA, will have decreasing influence as the years go by, because of the way world population is growing.

In 500 years' time, will it be the case that everyone will automatically be introduced to English as soon as they are born (or, by then, very likely, as soon as they are conceived)? If this is part of a rich multilingual experience for our future newborns, this can only be a good thing. If it is by then the only language left to be learned, it will have been the greatest intellectual disaster that the planet has ever known.

If there is a critical mass, does this mean that the emergence of a global language is a unique event, in evolutionary terms? It may be that English, in some shape or form, will find itself in the service of the world community for ever.

Further reading

For a much more detailed account of the English language, from the viewpoint of history, structure and social use, see my *Cambridge Encyclopedia of the English Language* (Cambridge: Cambridge University Press, 1995).

An introductory account of the language is Randolph Quirk and Gabriele Stein, *English in Use* (London: Longman, 1990). Another is Bill Bryson, *Mother Tongue: The English Language* (New York: William Morrow, 1990).

A textbook introduction to English is W. F. Bolton, *A Living Language: The History and Structure of English* (New York: Random House, 1982).

The impact of English on various countries is discussed in a series of essays in Richard W. Bailey and Manfred Görlach (eds.), *English as a World Language* (Ann Arbor: University of Michigan, 1982; Cambridge: Cambridge University Press, 1984).

The cultural history of English is well documented in Richard W. Bailey, *Images of English* (Cambridge: Cambridge University Press, 1991).

The diverse ways in which English language policy is developing is illustrated from six countries in Michael Herriman and Barbara Burnaby (eds.), *Language Policies in English-Dominant Countries* (Clevedon: Multilingual Matters, 1996).

An A-to-Z account of topics in English is Tom McArthur (ed.), *The Oxford Companion to the English Language* (Oxford: Oxford University Press, 1992).

Further reading

The periodical *English Today*, published by Cambridge University Press, reviews the field at quarterly intervals, with a great deal of attention paid to English as a world language.

Index